The Bible Was My Treasure Map

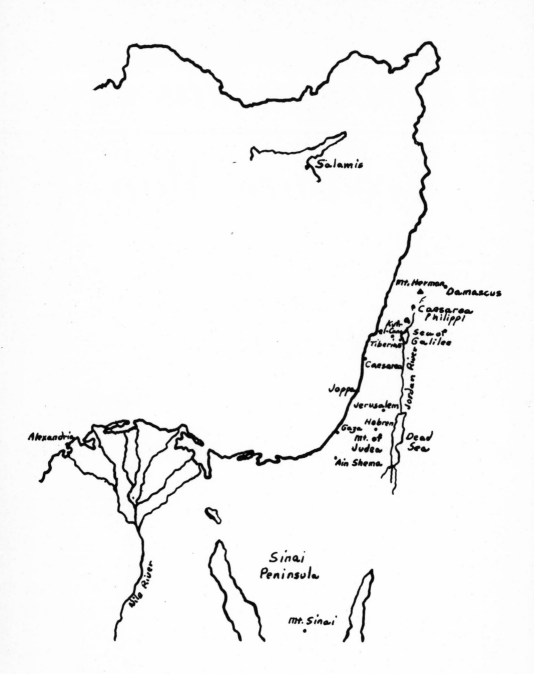

Salamis

Mt. Hermon
Damascus
Caesarea
Philippi
Kfr-
el-Cana
Sea of
Galilee
Tiberias
Jordan River
Caesarea
Joppa
Jerusalem
Hebron
Gaza
Mt. of
Judea
Dead
Sea
'Ain Shema

Alexandria

Nile River

Sinai
Peninsula

Mt. Sinai

The Bible Was My Treasure Map

by
Paul Ilton

Julian Messner, Inc.   New York

Published by Julian Messner, Inc.
8 West 40 Street, New York 18
Published simultaneously in Canada
by The Copp Clark Publishing Co. Limited

Endpaper illustration is a photograph of the pattern made by rolling in wet clay an Assyrian cylinder seal representing a priest between winged animals. This seal from Javneel, Palestine, dates to 400–200 B.C. and is a highlight of the Ilton collection.

Printed in the United States of America
Library of Congress Catalog Card No. 58-6019

To my wife, Sonja, and my son, Arie

Contents

Illustrations

Paul Ilton

Foreword

I have always felt that archaeology was born the hour man began to doubt the truth of the ancient scriptures and the Bible. Those archaeologists who have doubted were not necessarily irreligious men; I have yet to meet an atheistic archaeologist. These men believed, however, that blind faith was not enough to uphold the many questionable episodes of the Bible.

The great teachers who taught me to canalize my passion for the past brought me closer to God, for early in my career they encouraged me to practice archaeology with a special purpose: the confirmation of the Bible.

My own way was often unconventional, unorthodox. But my basic research before any excavation was systematic: I examined the known facts, the work of previous excavations, surveys of geographical areas, and blueprinted maps showing how towns, cities, houses, and tombs were built in ancient times, compared these with still existing ruins, remnants of walls, foundations, and even rock formations. Most important of all were the still existing written records in their original languages. But always the Bible was my first source of identification, and I became as intimate with its people as I was with my closest friends.

Paul Ilton

The Bible Was My Treasure Map

PART ONE

» I «

My Personal Obsession

I AM a free-lance archaeologist. I want to make this clear from the very beginning because the life of a scientist attached to a large expedition or foundation project is totally different from the unpredictable and frequently frightening adventures of an archaeologist out on his own. Actually, I am writing this first chapter after having finished the rest of the book, and I must confess that a good deal of what I have put down could easily have come from the pen of a Hollywood scenario writer with a good imagination. Yet it all happened pretty much as I have written it and I was probably more astonished than anyone as I read it back to myself. My life has been a far cry from what I thought it would be in 1925 when I made my first positive step toward tracking down the stories of the Bible with a pick and shovel.

Archaeology is one of the few fields left to the pioneer. The crust of the earth is fairly bulging with artifacts and relics of past civilizations waiting to be brought into the light, where they can provide us with the keys to many puzzling mysteries. From the discoveries of archaeology we have learned that civilizations and cultures never die or are forgotten in the strictest sense. The more we unearth, the more we see how ancient civilizations have had a subtle but unmistakable impress and bearing upon our lives today.

Man's psychology through the centuries has been unchanged. Both archaeology and anthropology have proved to us that man, at least since the dawn of recorded history, has not altered in his mental and emotional capacities. Recorded history as such began with the Bible, certainly the most comprehensive history of mankind ever written. Since the days of the Bible, man's social orders have changed and he has made tremendous technological advancements, but in broad terms what the ancients lived, suffered, and witnessed is the same as what we live, suffer, and witness today; nor, in essentials, is man's attitude toward the mysteries of existence fundamentally a different one. We have few thoughts that have not been thought before; there is none of our modern customs and traditions that does not have its roots in the past.

I can't remember exactly when it became my personal obsession to link the present with the past. While still a boy in Cologne, Germany, I was fascinated with the concept of archaeology, but it was only later that I realized I must go to the Bible for a real understanding of the ways and passions of men. And, discovering Biblical archaeology through the Bible, I found it the open sesame not only to knowledge but to faith. I recall reading avidly the writings of famous scientists who had devoted themselves to the confirmation of the Bible's eternal truth. Whenever a new and important archaeological find was announced I tried to obtain records and photographs of it. I daydreamed constantly about the people of the Bible, and tried to understand their lives and their deeds.

I suppose I was a stone's throw from entering the clergy, but as it turned out my life has brought me much of the satisfaction of a career in religion plus the added inspiration of physical contact with the substance of the Bible. It is my aim in these pages to convey some of the tremendous excitement of archaeology in the Holy Land. Out of the literally hundreds of objects I have found, perhaps only a small percentage are of major archaeological importance, yet each, regardless of its monetary or scientific value, has meant a great deal to me as an individual. When I hold in my hand a jar from the time of Samuel, or a broken piece of masonry that may offer additional proof of the existence of a civilization at a place and during a period that is identical with a description from the Bible, the very fact that I have uncovered another weapon against the skepticism and cynicism that have become fashionable is a source of tremendous gratification.

A few of the stories in this book are here primarily because I couldn't bear to leave them out. They are entertaining, I hope, even if their historical and Biblical significance is small. And, after all, isn't an author entitled to include a favorite or two even if they do not fit exactly under the title of his book or into the main purpose of his life?

» II «

Munim's Prophecy

APRIL 17, 1925. As the liner docked in Alexandria I searched for the ruins of the Pharos of Alexandria, built two thousand two hundred years ago by Ptolemy and his wife Arsinoë as a harbor guide. I was vastly disappointed. The Pharos in Ptolemy's day may have been the seventh wonder of the world, but now it impressed me as little more than a sun-bleached heap of stones.

From the dust-choked docks came the deafening din of construction. Legions of crippled beggars lined the quays, some of them eating from withered fingers the decayed food in their copper bowls. Sweating, coal-black Nubians carried heavy bales of cotton to and from the freighters. From the hundreds of small boats and barges surrounding the ship, colorfully dressed Egyptian and Sudanese merchants held up their cheap trinkets and screamed for the attention of the passengers. Gesticulating, naked Arab boys stood poised on the gunwales to dive for coins tossed down by the tourists. All was dirt, stench, and poverty; only the blue and brilliant sky above was clean.

My heart sank. Was this the land of the Nile, the fabled realm of the Pharaohs? I had been prepared to play the role of the awed foreigner in a country of vast and intimidating dignity, and now I found Egypt had no dignity at all, but shared the all-pervasive cheapness of the modern world.

My naïveté, of course, was unjustified. I had forgotten I was in the third decade of the twentieth century. The world was still recovering from the Great War; Egypt was yet to achieve political freedom, and the Egyptian royal family was unconcerned with the welfare of its people. In more recent years I have returned to Alexandria often, and time has made me more patient. Today it is hard for me to remember what wonders I had hoped to see, entering this raucous metropolis of the Mediterranean shore for the first time.

Though I had planned to spend some time at the Graeco-Roman Alexandrian ruins, I left the next morning for Cairo. I was in Egypt at the age of twenty-one as a foreign correspondent for the *Berliner Tageblatt*, a prominent paper that had hired me on the recommendation of the editor of a Cologne newspaper for which I had worked briefly. My one goal in life was to get to North Africa and the Middle East, and I had even studied Arabic to prepare myself. Just what I expected to do when I got there I can't quite recall, but I knew that just being there was half the battle won.

My interview with Theodore Wolff, chief editor of the *Tageblatt*, had involved a considerable amount of truth-stretching, but somehow my conscience refused to bother me. Wolff had asked me how often I had been to Africa and I had answered casually, "Oh, three or four times." I wonder today whether he was as taken in by this as he pretended to be. But the interview was successful and I was in Egypt at last. My salary was very small, but I would have plenty of free time to explore the countryside.

In Cairo my first obligation was toward Wolff and the editors of the *Tageblatt*. For a week I stayed close to the *pension* and wrote my first articles on Egyptian current events. Most of my information I got from reading the Egyptian newspapers, and my knowledge of the Arabic language helped me considerably. I wrote to people I wanted to interview, but put off mailing the letters. I was much more interested in meeting archaeologists.

In 1925 it was necessary for reporters in Egypt to obtain credentials from the Egyptian Ministry of the Interior. I went to the Ministry Building and was taken to the office of an Egyptian official, Ibrahim Bey Adham. Adham spoke French. He was friendly but noncommittal, and he seemed none too impressed by the genus European reporter.

"What can I do for you?" he asked me crisply. Adham was a short man, expensively dressed, with dark eyes, expressive hands, and a light brown complexion.

I told him of my assignment.

"How long do you expect to be in Egypt?" he asked. "One week, two, three?"

"Several months," I said. "Perhaps several years. It all depends."

He rolled his eyes ironically. "This is quite unusual. Most foreign writers are able, in less than a week, to learn enough about us, both past and present, to write a three-hundred-page book."

I laughed. "For years I have been studying Egyptian history, and still I know nothing about it."

He seemed pleasantly surprised, but with a faint trace of sarcasm continued. "Then you are well qualified to write about us, are you not?"

"Hardly. I have much more to learn, Excellency, and I would not write of your country till I had lived here for quite some time."

At this Adham became perceptibly more cordial. He finished looking over my credentials and turned to me, smiling. "You see, Ilton, when you love Egypt as I do, when you have my pride of country, in a job like this you have the right to a little bitterness. It is my responsibility to protect Egypt from hasty writers of travel books and journalistic "interpretations," and among foreign newsmen and writers you are a decided exception. These men would do Egypt harm by their ignorance and superficial opinions. Egypt can be understood only by those who understand her past as well as her present."

"Excellency," I said, "can it be you are an archaeologist?"

He shook his head. "Archaeology is a special science, and an art. The skill and knowledge it requires have not been given to me."

I wanted to prove to Adham I was not one of his superficial foreigners, though the articles I had written on Egypt before leaving Berlin were a source of guilt. My spoken Arabic was far from perfect, but the next words I addressed to him were in his native tongue.

I have never seen so sudden a change in a man's behavior. Jumping up from his chair, Adham embraced me in the traditional Egyptian manner, kissing both my cheeks. "I shall help you to discover Egypt!" he said, and without further ado invited me to dinner that night at Cairo's most famous Arabic restaurant, El-Hatti.

"You will not mind," he said at the door, "if one of my closest friends joins us? You will like him — he is not only my friend but my teacher, and a man of rare wisdom."

Ibrahim Bey Adham was waiting at El-Hatti when I arrived. "I have already ordered for us," he greeted me cordially. "We shall dine like the Pharaohs. My friend Munim is not here yet, but he is never late. Let us go to our table."

As we sat down Adham said, "There, you see, Munim is never late."

I turned to see a tall, slender Coptic priest coming toward our table. His skin was a shade darker than Adham's, and he had a small spade beard and deeply set eyes that flashed like black diamonds. His forehead was extremely high, his face ascetic. His long black robe rippled about him. As Adham introduced us his eyes looked searchingly into mine. "Welcome," he said, with a smile of extraordinary charm and beauty.

During dinner Adham kept the talk light and inconsequential. But with the coffee our conversation took a more serious turn. We discussed the recently discovered treasure of Tutankhamen and the excavations of Carnarvon that had revealed to the world the splendors of the Pharaohs. For the first time in my life I was with friends who shared my interest in the past, and we spoke of civilizations long since vanished as intimately as if we had been recalling college days.

I was so impressed by Munim that soon I was confiding my secret ambition to him. He nodded gravely at my enthusiasm and told me of an archaeologist friend who through his work had been able to confirm much of the Bible. When this man returned from England Munim would introduce me to him.

"His name," said Munim, "is Flinders Petrie. He is world-famous. But before you meet him, Paul, prepare yourself by seeing and learning as much as you can."

"I shall," I said solemnly and, in a superstition of my youth, I rapped the table.

Munim smiled. "Knocking wood is one of our old Oriental customs. Once we believed wood was inhabited by eternal spirits, and that these spirits must be appeased if good luck were to come our way. . . . But I had not realized how late it was," said Munim to our Egyptian host. "I shall see Paul home."

We said goodnight to Adham and left the restaurant.

On our way to my *pension* Munim asked if I had seen Ibn Taloun, Cairo's twelve-hundred-year-old mosque. I had not, and since the night was warm and clear, Munim suggested we walk there. We took seats on one of the stone benches beneath the towering columns. I felt warmly toward this striking man who had now fallen silent, as if in meditation; I wanted very much to be his friend. Munim's profundity and knowledge would be of great aid and inspiration to me. Here was one man who would only encourage my passion for the past.

Finally Munim spoke. "Among the ancient Egyptians were very wise men, men better versed in psychology than some of our most outstanding teachers and scientists. They had the gift of reading the future. They called the soul that emanates from every living creature the *ka*, and they could read this *ka*. In many old scriptures it is written that the *ka* cannot lie. I am able to know and advise you, Paul, because it is given to me to be able to read your *ka*."

This embarrassed me somewhat but Munim only smiled in the darkness. "In your lifetime you will witness many things beyond the realm of the ordinary. Many secrets shall be revealed to you. Doubtless, Paul, you will have many questions. Feel free always to call upon me if you wish answers. What answers I have I shall give you." He gave me his hand. "I am glad to be your friend."

We left the ancient mosque that lay bathed in moonlight. There were many questions I already wanted to ask, but sensing Munim's mood I was silent. At the *pension,* Munim made a gesture of blessing with his hands and left me.

The next week I was busy with my interviews of people important in Egyptian political life. I met Nahas Pasha, leader of the revolutionary Wafd party, one day to overthrow the government. I spent an afternoon with the fiery widow of Zaghlul Pasha, a commanding woman who crusaded for women's rights. Nahum Effendi, chief Rabbi of Egypt, told me of the ascendant Zionist movement in Palestine.

I wrote my articles quickly and dispatched them to Berlin. Now I was free! I spent hours at the Egyptian Museum, at the mummy cases, puzzling over hieroglyphic writing on slabstones. The wealth of the Egyptian past bewildered me. But nothing gave me as much pleasure as a single fragment of silk material, once part of the dress of a noblewoman in the time of Joseph. For me this scrap of material, representing a real life, recaptured the feel and atmosphere of the time. It had more meaning for me than the most impressive sarcophagus.

One day I was standing before the glass case in which the scrap of silk was exhibited. A museum guard tapped me on the shoulder to remind me that it was closing time but I had an after-hours appointment with Professor Alan Rowe, the British archaeologist in charge of the Museum's scarab and hieroglyphic section.

A secretary showed me into Rowe's small and cluttered office. Hundreds of stone tablets with hieroglyphic writings were scattered around. On the desk was a huge assortment of scarabs, bones, stones, or gems carved in the form of a beetle. Behind the desk sat Professor Rowe.

"How do you do," he said. "I have heard good things of you. You come highly recommended by my friend Munim."

I was startled. Since he had left me a week ago at the door of my *pension* I had not heard from Munim, and Munim had no way of knowing I had planned to get in touch with Alan Rowe.

Rowe knew I was a journalist interested in archaeology. Without preamble he shoved a large scarab across the desk. "This is the first scarab ever found from the period of Amenhotep IV. It bears his seal."

Knowing little of scarabs, I found it difficult to share Rowe's enthusiasm, but he listened with cordial understanding as I told him of my interest in archaeology. I left the Museum with two of his books and an invitation to drop by whenever I was able.

I took the trolley to the Pyramids the next afternoon. I approached the massive structures as shrines, reverently touching the ancient sand and limestone. But no exaltation seized me; I was completely and utterly unmoved.

The Pyramids were cold and silent; they told me nothing. Where were the secrets Munim had spoken of? I walked over a thousand yards of sand to the monumental Sphinx, hoping its mystery, its majesty, would strike some spark within me. I might just as well have looked at the sky or desert wastes.

Alexandria had shocked me with its crudeness of the present, but at the Pyramids I had been untouched by the remoteness of the past. I began to doubt my fitness for the work I planned to undertake.

Back in Cairo, I put through a call to Munim. He had left for his native Addis Ababa and would be away for another ten days. I called Adham; he, too, was out. I was too shy to get in touch with Alan Rowe.

Slowly, disheartened, I returned to the practicalities of life. Among the mail on my desk was a letter from the Swiss-Egyptian Company, a corporation that owned Egypt's most exclusive hotels. It was an invitation to spend a week, all expenses paid, at the Kataract Hotel in Aswan. The Kataract at this time was the world's most luxurious hotel. Only the very rich could afford its rates; Swiss-Egyptian must have thought there were a good many wealthy Germans among my readers. This was a welcome opportunity of escape from Cairo, and I accepted by telegram.

I took the night train for Aswan that evening. The train ran along the banks of the Nile, and watching the great river as it flowed in its eternal course helped me forget my loneliness. At the Kataract I was properly impressed, as a young man should be, by the silver and crystal and smart young women, but I was soon out in search of antiquity. The hotel was near the famous Valley of the Kings, with its colossal statue of Ramses and its tombs bedded deep in the sandstone of the mountains. Making my way through the tunnels of the three- and four-thousand-year-old grave chambers, it was as though I had left the contemporary world behind, to breathe the rarer air of other centuries and epochs.

I avoided the wealthy tourists. I spent most of my time among the ruins, and the chain that linked me to the past was strong again. I had seen the tombs of kings and queens who were contemporaries of the patriarchs of the Bible. I had walked on soil trod by Jacob, and seen ornaments and designs the Patriarch had seen when he and his sons had come to visit Joseph. The Biblical past had become vibrantly alive to me. In Aswan and the Valley of the Kings I had found myself again.

I spoke to the natives, men and women who had never left their place of birth. Despite their poverty and pitifully low standard of living, some of them, I found, reflected their country's past greatness. One farmer, old and poor, had two wives and twelve children, all of whom he supported on about twenty-five dollars a year. He and his family lived in a hut made from flattened-out oil tins discarded by the hotel. As I spoke with him two elegant women from the Kataract rode by on well-groomed horses.

I asked the old farmer, "Doesn't such wealth around you make you envious?"

"Envious?" He was surprised. "God gave me a body and a soul. What more do I need?"

"Perhaps you're right. But wouldn't a little money help?"

He shook his head. "We're all equal. We enter the world naked, and naked we leave it. Allah has made my life the way it was meant to be."

Was this resignation, contentment, or fatalism? At twenty-one I was too young to know the right answer, but the philosophy of this old Arab impressed me.

The next day I went to the little village of El-Shallala. Six miles from Aswan, El-Shallala is the last stop on the railroad; from it ships leave for Wadi Halfa and the Sudan. I strolled through the bazaar, sniffing the strong fragrances of the spice shops. At the little inn I drank a cup of strong, aromatic coffee. With nearly two hours to kill, I walked along the banks of the Nile, watching the fishermen who slept in the sun while the women mended their nets. Near the river was a cluster of some fifteen huts. Farmers knelt in the water washing their cattle — the gray *zamouses*, the heavy cows of Egypt. After leaving the river bank, I passed among the huts. Suddenly an old man stepped from behind one of the low clay buildings, blocking my path.

"*Saidi Chawadjah*," he said, greeting me in friendly Arabic. The man's face was deeply wrinkled, his body bent. He was dressed in rags.

I returned his greeting and made as if to pass, but he continued to stand in my way.

"I have something for you," the old man said. Under his arm was a longish object wrapped in old Egyptian newspaper.

"I don't want to buy anything," I told him, and backed away, reaching for some coins in my pocket.

The old man removed the newspaper from his package, and held the mummy of a child up to my face. I almost screamed at the dried hair, the parchment-like forehead, the protruding skeleton of a foot.

The old man muttered, "She died in the great famine. She was prepared for eternity, and now she is yours."

"Take it away," I said sharply.

But he persisted wheedlingly, "It is for you, my friend. Take it."

Despite my horror, I found it difficult to tear my eyes away from the child's face in its bindings of linen strips. From the lower gray-brown bindings hung a single object, a gold *ankh* cross *(crux ansata)*, the symbol of never-ending life. I stared at the *ankh*, both repelled and fascinated.

"Refuse me," he began anew, "and refuse what I offer you. But there is one thing you cannot refuse, your *ka*."

Here again was Munim's *ka*. I threw some coins at his feet, pushed past him, and walked rapidly away from the village. His fading words followed me: "You can't escape your destiny, for from destiny there is no escape. . . ."

That night I slept badly, and the next day on the train back to Cairo I was badly fatigued. The two-day train trip seemed like seven, and over and over again, like some unholy litany, I heard the old man's parting cry.

I telephoned Munim from the Cairo station and asked if he was free to see me. We agreed to meet in an hour at Shepheard's Hotel. At the *pension* I unpacked, bathed quickly, and hurried off to our appointment. Munim was waiting on the terrace.

"How was your trip?" he asked me, smiling.

I told him of the Valley of the Kings and my experience at El-Shallala. I asked if I had done wrong in refusing to buy the old man's grisly wares.

"Some day, Paul," said Munim, "you will return to El-Shallala. The old man was right. You cannot escape your *ka*."

"Really, Munim," I laughed. "This is nonsense."

"You are mistaken," said Munim evenly.

"But I cannot accept fatalism in so obvious a form."

Munim's eyes probed mine. "If God has set the stars so steadfastly in their orbits, why should he allow you, a human being, to wander aimlessly? I do not say your future is rigidly predetermined. But I do say it is up to you to accept or reject your opportunities, and so shape that future closer to your heart's desire. This old man could not understand why you refused from him something important to the fulfillment of your destiny."

"How," I demanded, "could this old man grasp things about me I don't even know about myself? No human being has that power."

"Read the prophets. Understand the real meaning of Jesus' teachings;

· 29 ·

and you will cease to be an unbeliever in the power of the unknown."

"Munim, what you consider theology, I consider superstition."

Munim shook his head. "What is it you wish to do with your life, Paul? Once you told me it was your purpose to seek out the truth. Your approach was the right one, for you found that truth in the Bible. Read the Bible closely and you will find that other truth of which I speak."

"Munim, I am confused. What am I to do?"

"Resolve your doubts, and become an archaeologist."

"But the years of study, Munim. The endless years of preparation. . . . I am no longer a child, just embarking on my education."

Munim smiled. "All men are children. There is no time that is not also opportunity, and a man is never too old to learn. I believe the old man was right, Paul, and that one's destiny is inescapable. You have told me your obsession is the past, and the past will also be your future. Since the night we met I have felt there is something different about you, and now I perceive that your difference from other men is this strange spiritual link you have with the past."

He pressed my arm. "For you the things of the past shall glitter and become alive. That is your destiny, Paul. Follow it."

"Then I must change my entire life."

It was as if he had not heard me. "Paul," Munim said, "why not go to Palestine?"

"Palestine?"

"You love and respect the Bible, and know it well. Go to the land where the Bible was lived. Somewhere there you will find what you are looking for."

"But my assignment, unfortunately, is to Egypt. I am not free financially to do as I please."

He shrugged and said, "God opens the door." He rose from the table. "Come see me Tuesday evening of next week, if you can."

I strolled alone through the warm night back to my *pension*. The conversation with Munim had relieved me, and I could think now of the old man of El-Shallala without fear or apprehension. Perhaps Munim was right, and I should change my profession. I wanted nothing more, yet it seemed impossible.

Three days later, returning to the *pension*, I found a telegram slipped under my door. It was from my editor in Berlin, and it read: POLITI-CAL EVENTS IN PALESTINE AROUSING GREAT INTEREST HERE. LEAVE IMMEDIATELY FOR JERUSALEM. WILL IN-STRUCT FURTHER THROUGH CONSULATE.

I sank weakly to the bed, remembering Munim's parting words: "Come see me next week, if you can." Before going to bed that night I prayed, and never before have I felt so close to God. "God opens the door," Munim had told me, and he was right.

» III «

City of Holiness

LIKE Rome, Jerusalem is bedded in valleys between its seven hills.
On the east is the Valley of Kidron, and above Kidron the Mount
of Olives; on the west and south Wadi er-Rababi bounds the Holy City,
meeting the Valley of Kidron near the Pool of Siloam. The city is like
a white diamond set in the majesty of the Judean Hills.

Walking through the narrow streets I could see Mount Moriah, where
Abraham had readied his sacrifice, and where Solomon built the first
great temple to Yahweh. I saw Mount Zion and in the further distance
the mount where Christ defied Satan.

I followed the narrow alleys of the bazaars to the Mosque of Omar,
third most holy shrine in the Moslem world. Built about seven hundred
years ago and named after the second Caliph Omar, the Mosque stood
on ground once occupied by the Temple of Solomon and the Synedrion
of the time of Christ. Its blue mosaics and bronze cupola are landmarks
in Jerusalem. I paused before that part of the ancient temple walls
where Jews still mourn their tragic past, and went to the Church of the
Holy Sepulchre, where the Christians worship.

In Jerusalem the old and new worlds mingle as the waters of two
great rivers. People from every corner of the earth have come here,
prodigal sons by the thousands, to await the opening of a magic door.

Jerusalem is both a dream and the answer to a vision.

In the faces of Jerusalem's Jews I saw the dream of Zion. For some Jerusalem was their native land; for others it was the land of their fore-fathers upon which they had laid a spiritual claim. These were the men and women who had fled persecution. Faces out of the Old Testament, wearing long beards and sideburns, they waited for the coming of the Lord. For them the ancient prayers were more important than the new plows and harrows the young Zionists so eagerly awaited. The old men dreamt not of the land, but of the Lord.

The faces of the Christians held another dream — life eternal. I saw it in their eyes, lowered in reverence, as they walked the Via Dolorosa, knelt in the Garden of Gethsemane, stood in veneration at Mount Calvary. The monks in their woolen robes, some white, some brown, some black, knew their dream would find fulfillment both for those they saved and for themselves. Their fate was with Christ and their task to spread His eternal Gospel.

I saw, too, the dream of the Moslems. In the fierce, implacable eyes of ascetic Bedouins I saw it; in the faces of Arab sheiks, golden daggers flashing at their waists; in the almond eyes of the beautiful women of Damascus, of Amman, and the vast deserts. They dreamed that once again Allah would punish the infidel and return to them their land.

I had arrived in Jerusalem on a Friday, the Sabbath of the Moslems. The next day, Saturday, was the Sabbath of the Jews, and the next the Sabbath of the Christians.

That Friday I watched thousands of Arabs pass through the winding streets of the bazaar. I followed their procession to the Mosque of Omar. Many *fellahin* were there from the nearby villages, as well as Bedouins of the desert with their daggers and scimitars. These men came from the Transjordan desert, the Dead Sea villages, and from Hebron, the town where Abraham once lived. I waited as they went to their prayers, then rejoined them in the bazaars. All the shops were busy, thronged by a festive, cheerful crowd.

Shortly before sundown the scene changed dramatically. Many shops closed and the narrow streets fell silent. Out of the old houses came the Orthodox Jews wearing their finest caftans, colorful long-sleeved garments tied at the waist by a girdle. The women were bedecked like brides of the Sabbath, their heavy silken robes rustling with every step. Off the Jews hurried to their houses of worship, many of these still situated in catacombs and cellars dug in the days of the Maccabees.

All the next day the Holy City was quiet, until sundown, when the Jews returned to their daily work. And on the next day silence reigned again in Jerusalem. But soon enough this silence was broken by the ringing from the chapels and churches of Christendom of hundreds of bells. The Christians began to celebrate their day of rest. Catholic processions of priests in jeweled copes, of monks and nuns, eyes fixed to the crosses in their hands, passed through the same streets to their holy places. The Protestants, carrying their thick Bibles, gathered on steps of their churches.

That afternoon I returned to the fortification ruins. It was here Jeremiah upbraided King Zedekiah and the people of Judea for betraying their God, and here the Babylonians of Nebuchadnezzar had wreaked their destruction. On this very spot, in 168 B.C., the Hebrews defied the Seleucid King, Antiochus IV (Epiphanes). And here, too, Jesus chased the moneychangers from the temple.

I stood surrounded by three thousand years of history, and the magnitude of what had occurred here was as thrilling to me as if I had witnessed it myself. Fleetingly aware of the bustle around me, lost in contemplation, I forget how long I stood there on those hallowed steps.

That evening I visited my friend Adolph Reifenberg. Reifenberg had been a fellow student at the University of Berlin. Now, at the University of Jerusalem, Adolf taught geology, but strangely his residence here had made of him an ardent numismatist. After I had told Adolf about my plans he said, "Come, I have something to show you," and getting up from the table, he led me to his study. There he spread a velvet cloth on the table and from the drawer took a small box. One by one, he displayed his magnificent collection of ancient coins. They were gold, silver, and bronze. There were silver shekels from the Maccabean era, coins from the time of the Procurators, from the reign of Pontius Pilate. The history of Palestine from the time of Alexander the Great to the destruction of Jerusalem was spread out before me on Adolf's table.

"So many coins," I said. "How did you find them?"

Adolf made an offhand gesture. "The Arabs are always finding them when they farm or build, and I have many friends among the Arabs." This was an archaeological trade secret I later put to good use.

I left Adolf's house that night with a letter of introduction to Professor Sukenik, head of the Archaeological Department of the newly founded Hebrew University of Jerusalem. Among Sukenik's finds, all of them excavated in the vicinity of Jerusalem, I saw Roman marble sarcophagi, bronze daggers, Assyrian cuneiform tablets, a pair of gold earrings worn probably by a Jewish noblewoman in the days of the second temple, mosaics excavated from synagogues of the Byzantine period.

Though interesting, these antiquities did not compare with those I had seen in the Cairo Museum. Sukenik told me his department was new and lacked the funds necessary for large-scale archaeological research. For more than fifty years outstanding objects had been found in Palestine, but under the Ottoman regime most of them had been sent to the British Museum in London and to other museums the world over.

"New York's Metropolitan Museum and the Louvre in Paris have more Palestinian antiquities of the Biblical period than we will ever find. You see how poor we are, and one cannot dig without money. But one day," he said emphatically, "one day we will have our own museum, and it will astonish the world."

Sukenik's attitude struck me as somewhat materialistic and utilitarian. For him Biblical archaeology had but one purpose, to glorify the Jews and Palestine. The job of his department was to prove the greatness of the early Hebrew nation. He was indifferent to the discovery

· 35 ·

of antiquities of Babylonian, Assyrian, Greek, or Roman origin. It was hard for me to accept Sukenik's chauvinism, but despite our differences we became good friends.

That day I rented a small four-room house in the Christian Arab quarter of Musrara. My landlord found a servant for me, a young Arab boy from Bittir named Mahmud. Mahmud had served previously in the household of a British official, and came with good references.

In the following weeks I became better acquainted with ancient Jerusalem. The old city was like a mirror held to the past. Many of the houses near the Mosque of Omar and the Wailing Wall still stood on Roman and Hebrew foundations. Archways connecting houses bore the chisel marks of Greek, Roman, and Byzantine masons. Over these pavements, scarred and worn, the prophets had once walked.

I felt at home in the ancient streets and quarters. Only three months had passed since I had left Germany, yet my immediate past had, to me, the substance of a dream. In the Holy Land I had found the air sweetest to my lungs, the food that satisfied my soul.

At the American School of Oriental Research I listened with open mind to the lectures of its archaeologists, and through them became increasingly familiar with the methods of modern Biblical archaeology, its exacting research, its careful excavation, recording, and speedy publication. I read the books my new archaeological friends recommended, but in a helter-skelter, unsystematic way, the result of my desperation to absorb as much information and learning as possible in the shortest time. What I needed was a mentor-teacher willing to direct my studies programmatically.

It soon became apparent to me that the study of archaeology required the mastering of several related sciences. History, including under its rubric religion, art, invention, fashion, economics was only the first of these. Archaeology is also related to anthropology, since no archaeologist can ignore what the anthropologist can tell him of the culture and psychology of various races from ancient up to modern times. The archaeologist must also be familiar with geology; knowledge of the geological formations of an excavation site is of the first importance. The connection between archaeology and architecture is a close one; without trained architects and surveyors in the field the archaeologist cannot secure reliable plans on which excavation is based, and knowledge of the architecture with which peoples built their first houses and places of worship is essential, since each period has its specific type and kind of buildings. The design of a Babylonian temple is different from that built by the Assyrians. In the temple of Solomon we find Phoenician influences. The Egyptian pyramid was influenced by the early Babylonian ziggurat (temple-tower). Greek and Roman temples have their origins in all of these. The huge Egyptian pillars of the temple of Karnak in Luxor are reborn in the elegance of the Doric pillars of the Greek temples of Aphrodite.

A knowledge of how the men of early civilizations handled the problems of engineering is also important to the archaeologist. Long before the Roman viaducts, the Babylonians and Assyrians had elaborate systems of drainage in their palaces and in their cities of Nineveh and Ur. Copper plumbing was known in the Mycenaean period (1500-1100 B.C.); King Kronos of Crete had an intricate system of palace baths. The knowledge of chemistry is another *sine qua non* for the archaeologist, for chemical substances of the earth produce a patina or overlay, which in its various colors establishes the identity of objects dug from the ground. Silver becomes overlaid with a purple-violet patina; glass, red-green, gold, or silver; bronze, green or red, according to the soil in which the objects were buried or entombed. Only gold never deteriorates or changes regardless of how long or where it is buried.

These are some of the sciences with which the archaeologist must become familiar, for not only does he dig for relics; his task is to reconstruct the society of men as it once existed in all its complexity and diversification.

Discouraged by the enormity of the task ahead of me, I was overcome by loneliness and dissatisfaction. In the next weeks I made two friends who helped me during this difficult period when I frequently considered giving the whole thing up and returning to Germany. Father Fleurant, of the Monastery of St. Anne in the Via Dolorosa, was librarian of the Franciscans in Jerusalem. He was also curator of the monastery's small museum of archaeological relics. Though less learned than my other archaeological friends, he was intelligent and understanding. Through him I met his constant companion, Rabbi Ben-Goral, a young man of great warmth and enthusiasm.

I often wished Munim was in Jerusalem to join in our discussions. My letters to him at his church in Cairo had gone unanswered, so I knew he was in Addis Ababa. Munim had promised me an introduction to Flinders Petrie, and I waited impatiently for word from him.

Sir William Matthew Flinders Petrie was at this time the world's outstanding archaeologist. Petrie had uncovered the tombs of the first dynasty at Abydos, and the gravestones of Merneptah at Thebes, containing the earliest known Egyptian reference to Israel. In Palestine Sir Flinders had discovered the ten lost cities at Tell el-Hesy, south of Jerusalem. His books were fundamental to any study of antiquity. Independent by nature and habit, his connection with the universities was a loose one. At present Petrie was working on his new book, *Palestine and Israel*, which promised great advances in Biblical archaeology. To know Petrie would have meant much to me.

He lived in an Arab house surrounded by a well-kept garden in Abator, a quarter of Jerusalem on the eastern slopes of Mt. Zion, between the city and Bethlehem. Petrie had been described to me as both cordial and helpful, though he avoided those who might waste his time. I knew I was presuming, but when a week passed with no word from Munim I could no longer resist the temptation to call upon him.

I was shown into Petrie's study, where the great man was busy with his papers. I regretted my intrusion, but Sir Flinders made me at ease with a flash of his kindly blue eyes. He was a tall man, gray at the temples, tanned and slightly built. He had the unmistakable stamp of the British aristocrat. I liked him on sight.

"What can I do for you?" he asked me pleasantly.

"If you don't mind," I stammered, "I'd just like to talk."

He smiled. "And how should we begin?"

I pulled myself together. "Sir Flinders, that is precisely the question, and the reason why I have come to see you."

Petrie gave me a puzzled look, and I blurted, "I must become an archaeologist, and I don't know how to begin. That is — " I stopped, floundering in confusion.

"There is only one way to begin," said Petrie. "Study the Bible till you know it as intimately as the back of your hand. Read it in its most ancient versions, the Hebrew and the Aramaic. Then learn hieroglyphics. Study cuneiform and the geological formations. Then, if you are ready, and only if you are ready, dig."

He understood my discouraged silence. "The first requisite is patience," he went on. "What has been buried for thousands upon thousands of years can wait a few more years to be uncovered."

It was as if Munim sat before me. Like Munim, Petrie had the rare presence and authority of the man of faith, dedicated only to God and truth.

It seemed Petrie had taken a liking to me; we talked for hours, till Lady Petrie knocked on the door to remind Sir Flinders it was dinner time. They invited me to join them. Lady Petrie was her husband's co-worker in every sense of the word, and shared his love of archaeology; she accepted me warmly. They both had that rare spirit of understanding the world in terms of the past linked to the present and even to the future. In the Petries was a quality not only of breed and intellect but of the soul, that old-fashioned word in disrepute today, and it seemed to me that much of this quality of the soul had been fashioned by their work, dedicated and painstaking and idealistic.

I left their house that night determined to live the kind of life Sir Flinders lived. I still had doubts; I would be abandoning a promising writing career, would be destroying any immediate possibility of marriage and a family, would be cutting myself adrift from a safe and conventional course of life for what most people would consider a chimera. But I had at last made up my mind.

When I returned a few days later to the house in Abator, I was disappointed to find Sir Flinders out of the city. Lady Petrie invited me into the garden.

"Well," she asked, "have you reached your decision?"

"Yes."

She smiled. "I'm glad. Both of us have much confidence in you and your future."

Lady Petrie took a letter from the pocket of her dress. "This letter arrived this morning. It is from Munim, who speaks of you in glowing terms. I would take it as a good omen that you arrived before the letter, and in a sense made your decision independently of what influence it could have had upon my husband. Sir Flinders will be glad to help you, as much as he can."

I took the old lady's hand and pressed it, and our friendship was sealed.

» IV «

Baptism at Beth-shan

AT THIS time in his career Flinders Petrie was unoccupied with
field work, and I became his private pupil. For months I went to
his study three times a week, where I studied the sociology of ancient
times, art forms in pottery, the archaeological evolution of time, the
reading and understanding of history, the differentiation of layers of
civilization as to period, and — perhaps the most important of all —
where to sink the first spade and how to tell the genuine object from the
sham by a touch of the fingertips.

Dr. Hamilton of the Institute of Oriental Research was leaving shortly
to excavate near the town of Beisan in the valley of Esdraelon. Hamilton said he would be delighted to have me accompany him on the expedition. Sir Flinders, who did not want me to concentrate on book learning alone, urged me to go along with Dr. Hamilton and his associate
Dr. Iliffe.

"But let me give you a word of advice," he told me. "Keep your eyes
and ears open and your mouth shut. There is time in the future to offer
opinions. And take special notice of the Oxford method."

I had no idea of what the Oxford method was, but thought it better to see it for myself. A few days later the expedition party met at the old Jerusalem post office in the early morning hours. Including myself we were a party of twelve: Drs. Hamilton and Iliffe, two photographers, two experts in geology and chemistry, Helen Macloyd, an Englishwoman who had once worked with Flinders Petrie, an Arabic inspector from the Department of Antiquities and his Moslem factotum, who later proved useful as interpreter and liaison man between the Arab workers and scientists of the expedition.

In three hours' time our two cars had reached the plain of Esdraelon. After we passed the village of Zer-'In we saw before us the hill of Nebi-Dahi, identified by historians and archaeologists as the hill of Moreh. To the right was the low-lying plain called the Valley of Jezreel. In the center of this fertile plain, which extends to the River Jordan, is the town of Beisan.

Our road turned to the northeast, and a short time later we arrived at the Zionist colony of Affulah. The Zionists, who had bought large areas of the surrounding plain from the Arabs, hoped that one day Affulah would be an important agricultural center. From Affulah there was a good road leading to Beisan, thirteen miles away. This was my first trip through the landscape of the Bible, and I listened closely as my British friends connected the villages and topography with events in the Bible that had occurred thousands of years in the past. We made our way through the Arab settlement of Ain Jalud (Gideon's fountain), and I was surprised to hear from Helen Macloyd that the story of Gideon was still remembered here among the native people. I thought to myself that many other memories passed down from generation to generation must still be alive in these parts.

As we left behind the Jewish settlement of Ain Harod, I was reminded that what was now the site of a modern pumping station once had been a spring where Bedouins found refreshment. Another battle had been fought here seven hundred years ago between the Khwarizmian Mongols and the Egyptian Sultan Baibars, who in defeating the Mongols freed Palestine from its invaders. Many Egyptian Moslems, Hamilton told me, made an annual pilgrimage here.

We had but one more village to pass before reaching Beisan: the Jewish communal Beit Alfa, situated on the slopes of Gilboa. Here Professor Sukenik and other Hebrew scholars had found remains of a Jewish synogogue of the sixth century A.D. Subsequently excavated, the ruins had revealed fine mosaic floors with elaborate Biblical representations, and signs of the zodiac in fine tesellated designs. Aramaic and Greek inscriptions dated the floors from the time of Emperor Justinian.

Finally we entered the outskirts of Beisan, known in Biblical times as Beth-shan. During the time of the patriarchs the town, the ancient crossroads of Babylon, Damascus, and Jerusalem, had been important militarily and as a trade center. During the fifteenth century it had been the fortress of the Egyptian Pharaoh Tuth-moses III, whose governor ruled over the native Canaanites, a Semitic people who inhabited Palestine at the time of the Hebrew conquest *ca.* 1230 B.C. The Canaanites had built two great temples, one to Mekal, the city god of Beth-shan, the other to his female counterpart. Other temples had certainly existed; at least three temple ruins from the period had been found.

Beisan was an archaeologist's dream, for nine different levels of the city had been excavated previously, each of them richly revealing in Biblical history. Sacrificial instruments, figurines, and gold jewelry from this locale are in the British Museum and Jerusalem's Rockefeller Museum. They testify to the wealth and comfort in which people of the time lived under Canaanite-Hebrew rule.

The next stratum revealed the town of Ramses II and his successor, down to the period of approximately 950 B.C. Ruins of Canaanite temples of the same period had been discovered: one, the Temple of Dagon, dedicated to the god Reseph; the other dedicated to the goddess Astarte.

Other levels had shown traces of early Philistine, Israelite, and Assyrian cultures, among them a Philistine place of worship, the walls of an Israelite temple, and monuments to the Assyrian winged god Ashurshamesh. One of the latter can be seen in the British Museum.

Most probably an earthquake and the resulting fire had destroyed the city; pottery, brick, and stone found in the succeeding strata were charred and broken. Soon afterward the Hebrews, Greeks, and Romans had resettled Beth-shan, building magnificent houses, temples, and amphitheaters. In the early second century B.C. the Greeks renamed Beth-shan Scythopolis, after a Scythian tribe that had once invaded the city. The name "Scythopolis" occurs in the Septuagint of the Old Testament. In this era a Greek-Roman temple dedicated to Dionysus was important as a place of worship and the site for the annual commemoration of Spring; it attracted many from the nearby towns and villages of Esdraelon.

With the growth of Jewish power, Scythopolis in 107 B.C. passed into the hands of the Jewish high priest John Hyrcanus. It remained under Maccabean rule until forty-three years later, when Palestine became a Roman province.

In more recent levels of Beth-shan remnants of one of the first Christian circular churches, built after Constantine I recognized Christianity as the Roman religion in A.D. 330, have been found. Various other excavations revealed the important role the city played in the early and middle Byzantine periods as one of the pillars of nascent Christendom.

The Beth-shan excavations were an outstanding example of archaeological skill and method that had verified history known only through the Bible.

Before going to the site Hamilton and Iliffe had chosen, we had lunch in a little street *café* in modern Beisan. Many of the ruins of ancient Beth-shan and Scythopolis were now monuments in the modern quarter. In the market place opposite our *café* stood a black granite stele (obelisk) with hieroglyphic writing from the period of Pharaoh Seti I. Near the well stood a marble sarcophagus of exquisite Roman masonry.

As we rode to the site on the outskirts of the city, I reviewed in my mind the purpose of our expedition. During a hundred years of archaeo-

logical excavation in Beisan, little or nothing had been uncovered revealing the influence of early Babylonia. It was generally accepted that
in the Hebrew patriarchal period, around 1800 B.C., Babylonian influence must have been strong in Canaan; many Babylonian cuneiform
tablets had been found there. The Beth-shan that had been of importance
in Biblical history had assuredly been touched by Babylonian culture,
and we meant to find material evidence of it.

On Hamilton's site bricks had been discovered that had once belonged
to a Babylonian ziggurat (temple-tower). Unlike other Babylonian
bricks, those from Beth-shan bore no cuneiform writing, and the exact
date of their period could not be determined. It was entirely possible
that the bricks had been brought here from elsewhere by an Arab for
the building of a house the Arab had never completed. In this case, the
actual ruins of the ziggurat might be not on the site Hamilton had
chosen, but far distant from it.

Arriving at the site, our Arab helpers, who had been hired in the town,
put up our four tents that would serve as shelter. One of these I shared
with Dr. Iliffe. Another served as a study and workroom. Here, where
our photographic equipment, tools, files, and records were kept, the
Arabs set up folding chairs and tables.

Settled, we went back to look at the site area already fenced off with
rope for excavation. About forty by sixty feet in size, the north side of
the site was bounded by a natural formation of limestone rock greatly
deteriorated by rain and weather. The Babylonians had often used such
a natural outcropping as one of their temple walls. Hamilton believed
that within the roped-off area the ancient ruins of Babylonian brick
walls would be found.

We were on the site early next morning. When the workmen pushed
the first shovel into the ground we breathed a silent prayer. As we
turned over the surface, we found pottery shards of Arabic or late
Byzantine origin, but none that were Babylonian. The shovelfuls of
earth were poured into open baskets and carried by Arab girls and

women to the work tent, where the soil was examined carefully for more shards of pottery and brick. It was monotonous work as Hamilton, Iliffe, Helen Macloyd, and I sat on the ground sifting the dirt. At the site the Arab inspector supervised the digging, which together with the sifting continued till nightfall, interrupted only by lunch. The excavation ditch was now one foot deep and thirty-five feet long, and we had found nothing.

But neither Hamilton nor Iliffe was discouraged. Their calculations and blueprints told them this was the spot where the Babylonian ziggurat of Beth-shan had once stood. What made Hamilton's theory more plausible was the fact that some months before he had found, not far from the present site, a dried-out well in disuse for more than three thousand years. He believed Babylonian worshipers had used this well for ceremonial cleansing before entering the temple itself.

The next day we began photographing the site for an accurate record of our progress, and on the third day Hamilton ordered the crew to pickax the rock formation. No trace of man-made walls was found.

By the fourth day we had still accomplished nothing. If this was typical of archaeological field work, I found it dull and unrewarding. Perhaps I was too young for the virtue of patience. I looked for every shovelful of dirt to yield new discoveries; I found it hard to understand the confidence of my friends despite their failure. I left the site to stroll through the narrow streets of Beisan, talking to the people in the bazaar and sitting in the *café* at the market place, dreaming of Esdraelon's past.

One day I visited the ruins of a Canaanite temple. On its altar animals had been sacrificed and their blood offered up to the gods. The place had a magnetic power and aroused my imagination; I went to dream before it by the hour, forgetting both the expedition and the newspaper article that should have been claiming my attention.

There must, I thought, be a more profitable way of revealing the past than my friends at the site had been able to discover; perhaps modern archaeologists relied too heavily on scientific method and calculation.

I understood the need for practical photography, for blueprints, for careful research. But I wondered if scholars did not ignore a valuable source of information in the folklore of the natives — their stories, legends, and sagas that were part of the Bible. In talking to the people of Beisan I had been surprised to find that much of their folklore and legend was still alive. Most of these people could neither read nor write; but though illiterate, their knowledge of historical events was amazingly accurate. Facts we knew from ancient scriptures were part of their daily reference.

One old man told me that once the body of a king had been put upon the city walls to dry in the sun, and that the king's spirit had returned to take revenge upon his killers. I asked the old man if he knew the name of this king. "He had no name," he answered. "He was the King."

This was the story of King Saul, still alive three thousand years after his death. Many such legends were alive in the Holy Land, and I sensed that one day they might be the means through which I would find my own way of illuminating the truths of the Bible.

It was shortly before sunset that Friday afternoon when one of the workmen found half a brick in the excavation ditch. Hamilton examined the brick thoroughly and dipped one corner of it into water. In less than two seconds the wet portion had dried completely, proof that the brick was thousands of years old. It was of Babylonian origin, for analysis of the clay found it a combination of sand, straw, and mortar used exclusively by the people who lived on the Euphrates river. Hamilton's theory had been confirmed. It was extremely unlikely that this brick had been brought by Arabs to the site; in that case it would have been found closer to the surface of the ground.

Three more brick fragments were discovered the next morning. Discarding our shovels in our excitement, we dug the earth with our bare hands. Every bit of shard or clay found now was vitally important. But our enthusiasm soon waned, for the next brick fragments we found had burn marks, meaning that the temple had been destroyed by fire. Probably those bricks that had escaped destruction had been carried from the site and used for other buildings after fire had razed the temple. Though we now had sufficient evidence of the temple itself, the discovery of its exact location would require three times the number of Arab workmen we had to expand the site and dig to the temple foundations. The work would take at least seven months, and new funds would be needed for it.

The rope fences were left standing and two watchmen hired to prevent the local Arabs from treasure-hunting. The site was declared the property of the Department of Antiquities and we left for Jerusalem the next day.

So ended my first archaeological expedition.

At least five thousand pounds were needed to continue the excavation at Beisan, and four months would pass before Hamilton and the Institute of Oriental Research would be able to organize a new expedition. Once the temple foundations were unearthed important new discoveries would be made, and I could not understand the casualness with which everyone treated the delay. I would have continued to dig myself, alone. Flinders Petrie understood my eagerness, but warned me to be patient.

"It is money, Paul, that makes the world go round, and especially the archaeologist. There is a word I hate more than any other in the English language — the word "budget." Every institute, every organization has a budget, and we dangle like puppets at the end of its purse strings. If there is a budget we archaeologists can work and live; without one we can only write books and monographs." Petrie smiled, but I sensed his seriousness.

"We are totally dependent upon the good will of millionaires," Petrie went on. "Often I have thought that only rich men can afford to be archaeologists."

"Like Schliemann?"

"Schliemann was the one man who amassed his millions with a purpose. Only when he was rich and independent did he begin field work."

"There must be another way."

"Find it," smiled Petrie, "and archaeology will build a monument to your memory."

I wondered if I should tell Sir Flinders of my belief that with the clues of local folklore and legend many discoveries could be made without the time and expense of large-scale excavation? I decided against it. Who was I, the rankest neophyte, to plump for romantic unorthodoxy with this man who had inaugurated the new system of carefully planned excavation and recording in the minutest detail?

In the next years I spent long hours in study with Petrie and at my classes at the Hebrew University. There I immersed myself in Professor Meyer's course in ancient Hebrew, Aramaic, and various other Semitic idioms; demotic hieroglyphics, and the discoveries of Grotefend, who ninety years before had deciphered cuneiform writing. I gave little time to my journalism.

Munim had written congratulating me on my decision, and I heard from Alan Rowe, who made me feel closer to the fraternity by sending proofs of his forthcoming book. I was much in the stimulating company of Father Fleurant and Rabbi Ben-Goral. Thinking back on this period of my life, I see it as a time of hard work, good fellowship, and hope for the future. I was no longer the victim of my indecision; I had found my path, and meant to stick to it.

Shortly after the expedition to Beth-shan my life changed greatly for the better; I became a married man. Her name was Sonja, and she was a refugee borne to the Holy Land on the tides of the Russian Revolution. A dark beauty with eyes blue as the Lake of Galilee, Sonja spoke Russian and a little French; she could hardly understand my verbal ardors. Yet three days after our first meeting we were married.

Sonja took over Mahmud, my houseboy, and the little house on Musrara Street, bringing the feminine touch to my austere bachelor's quarters. She understood my passion for archaeology and quickly developed an interest in it; basically a religious person, the Bible had deep meaning for her. It was no time at all before she had completely reorganized my life. My books were catalogued, my papers stacked and filed, my study cleaned and brightened with fresh flowers daily. We entertained with regularity, and my social life took on a pattern and solidity possible only to the man who has received the approval of society.

We were frequent visitors to the American colony nearby, of which most of my friends from the school of Oriental Research were members. Discussions there with colleagues, friends, and priests of various denominations were fruitful for me. I had long since finished at the University; after a year I had been able to read ancient Hebrew and cognate Semitic languages, and these made it possible for me to understand the background behind much of the Biblical writings.

At the home of George Whiting, dean of the American colony, I made the acquaintance of a remarkable man, Olaf Madson, the Swedish archaeologist. Madson combined precise, scientific thinking with creative imagination; he was both an artist and a scholar. We became good friends and Madson, now curator of Stockholm's Royal Archaeological Museum, was a welcome addition to our discussions on the porch of my house in Musrara. In later years Madson's help was invaluable to me in discovering a marble head that may be of Salome, the Princess of Judea.

Jerusalem had become Sonja's and my second home. Its Biblical sites had become so familiar to me that I could find them even in the dark of night. I had learned through Adolf Reifenberg the secret of collecting and making friends with a number of Arab farmers on the outskirts of Jerusalem, and I urged them to show me what ancient relics they accidentally found. They had brought me a quantity of coins, and by now I had a fairly valuable collection of Greek, Roman, and Hebrew *dinars* and *aurei*. I was especially proud of three bronze pennies from the reign of Pontius Pilate. Whenever Arabs brought me such coins I would go with them to the site of discovery, make an exact drawing of it, and ask my Arab friends to tell me what stories and legends they knew about it. I would then compare these with similar stories and legends from the scriptures.

Flinders Petrie responded with the keenest interest when I showed him a quarter shekel I had received from an Arab farmer who had told me a story of Maccabean times connected with the area in which he had discovered the coin. Petrie was anxious to see the spot, believing that excavation there might uncover a Maccabean village or town. Unforeseen circumstances required that we drop the idea and it was forgotten. But Petrie's interest had spurred my own, and from then on I had more confidence in my own methods of detection.

One evening Father Fleurant, Rabbi Ben-Goral, Professor Madson, and I were discussing the strange names of Arab villages. We were talking in particular of Zorah, a small Arab village situated on a hill of the Southwest Judean mountains. The name "Zorah" was neither Arabic, Hebrew, nor Aramaic, but Assyrian. It meant "curled hair." McAllister's and Garsten's excavation in 1910 had revealed Zorah as the birth or dwelling place of Samson, the performer of Herculean exploits who had fought the Philistines and met his end at the hands of Delilah. The Arab village of today had preserved in its name an event that had taken place three thousand years before.

This had led me to conclude that other, more obscure, etymological discoveries might be made along the same lines, and I directed my studies toward this end. From the Department of Survey of Palestine's mandate government I got maps of regions mentioned in the Bible. The results were striking. The names of at least ten contemporary Arab villages were traceable to their Babylonian, Assyrian, Phoenician, ancient Hebrew, or Aramaic roots.

One village, Tell el-Qassīs, meant "Hill of the Priest" and had received its name from the conflict of Elijah against the priests of Baal. An adjoining village, Khirbet el-Dehab, meaning "Ruin of the Sacrifice," had been named for the same Biblical story. The illiterate Arabs were, of course, unfamiliar with both the Bible and these etymological facts. When I had compiled an entire list of Arabic place names traceable to Biblical events, I was sure I could find in at least some of these villages and towns material evidence of the Biblical past, evidence discoverable at small financial cost. With the advice of Father Fleurant, I chose Zorah for my first expedition. A German, Schumacher, had been the last to excavate there some twenty years before.

Early one August afternoon I left Jerusalem by train for Artuf, a village of the slopes of the Judean mountains from which Zorah was half a mile distant. These hills had once been populated by the Philistines in the time of the Judges, *ca.* 1100 B.C., and were the scene of constant skirmishes between the Philistines and the early Israelite settlers.

Previous archaeological expeditions had left their marks everywhere. Here were Canaanite ruins, there remnants of Philistine civilizations thousands of years old. In the fields I saw two marble pillars, the remains of a Greek temple. I knew Schumacher had uncovered a Canaanite temple courtyard and a stone altar. Some of the smaller pieces of bronze and pottery he had found were now in the British Museum.

From Artuf the road to Zorah was a narrow, rocky path up the hillside. It was eleven in the morning when I reached the town. Clustered before me were some twenty-odd small yellow-white clay houses. In their midst stood a well, fenced with chiseled stones at least two thousand years old. Beyond was a small white mosque with a ten-foot minaret. It was as though an illustration in the Bible stories I had read as a child had come suddenly to life.

An Arab friend, Affif el-Fastan, who was a goldsmith in Jerusalem, had given me the name of the village sheik, who proved to be cordial and anxious to help. After I introduced myself, he clapped his hands and women brought stools from the house and placed them in the shade. I told him that I would like to see the place where archaeologists had dug many years before.

The sheik rose, gave me directions, and returned to his house. I left the courtyard and made my way through the village to a terrace overlooking the valley. There I found the Canaanite ruins uncovered by Schumacher. The walls were completely crumbled. In the hillside caves were two chambers, once evidently the quarters of the priests but now piled high with rubbish thrown there over the years by the villagers.

It was here in these hills that the Hebrews under Joshua's leadership had settled after their exile from the land of Goshen in Egypt. Perhaps Joshua himself had stood where I now stood, waiting for the women of his tribe to bring him water from the village well. Here, too, the Canaanites had worshiped their idols, and taught the Hebrew seminomads the art of house construction. Here, later, the Hebrews had in turn taught the Canaanites to forget their gods and instead to worship Yahweh.

Not far from Zorah, a thousand yards below in the valley, lay another Arab village. Though its present inhabitants were ignorant of the fact, this village still held the name of King Saul who had once dwelt here within its walls. In the time of the Judges, some three thousand years ago, there had been constant intercourse between the two villages.

I was examining the temple altar when behind me I heard a stifled giggling. I turned to see several Arab boys. They made my first lecture audience, as I told them of the life that had once flourished in these hills. I described the townspeople as they paid their homage to the first Hebrew king, and to the prophet Samuel who had chosen and anointed him. I was perhaps long-winded, and my listeners deserved a reward. Sonja had packed hard candy in my knapsack, and I passed it around to the delighted children.

When I returned to the village, the sheik was waiting for me in the courtyard. "Do you know these boys?" he asked me.

"We talked at the temple," I said, rumpling the hair of a black-eyed six-year-old.

"They are my grandsons," he told me proudly. "Allah has been good to me. He gave me eighteen sons. The eldest is a grandfather himself." The sheik smiled broadly. "Spend the night with us, and in the morning you may dig."

He took me to his small herd of sheep, and with a regal gesture indicated that I should choose the one to be slaughtered for our evening meal. As I later learned, this was done in behalf of only the most honored guests.

At the banquet that night the sheik, a huge man of sixty with a bushy beard, was flanked by his six oldest sons and four village elders. The Arabs made their devotions before eating, facing toward Mecca and bowing their heads several times to the ground. Then the sheik prayed aloud, the others repeating after him. The ceremony took some thirty minutes. We used our fingers to eat the food placed before us in large pottery bowls.

As we ate we talked, and the elders told me stirring tales of their forefathers, tales no outsiders had heard before. We talked till the moon was high, and in these hours I learned more of Arabic customs and traditions than I had absorbed in years of reading. It was late when the sheik led me to the hut where I would sleep that night. The floor was of stamped earth; from the wall hung a blackened kerosene lamp. On the ground were two blankets. Inexperienced, I had brought no bedding with me. I took off my shirt, pulled up the blanket, and waited for sleep.

It came, but not for long. I woke to a terrible itching, and in the dim light saw squadrons of bedbugs. I jumped to my feet frantically and brushed them off, but I knew that with bedbugs an amicable partnership was impossible, and went outside to the dying open fire. There I huddled till dawn, dozing off at intervals.

By seven o'clock, accompanied by two Arab helpers, I was back at the Canaanite ruins. When we had emptied one of the two chambers of its rubbish I went inside to investigate, tapping the walls for hidden rooms and digging into the hard earth floor to determine if it was hollow. I searched everywhere for possible burial compartments, but found nothing. When the second chamber had been cleared of rubbish I searched it in a similar manner, but to no effect.

Then I remembered my cardinal error. "What did you do with the rubbish from the first chamber?" I asked the men. They pointed to a heap a few feet away. They laughed when I began a painstaking search through the rubbish, but stopped when I found two pottery vessels.

"Why did you throw these away?" I demanded.

"Why not?" said one. "They are nothing."

They were a great deal — clay jars from the time of the Judges,

1250-1000 B.C. About the size of a man's palm, the jars were of the grayish-brown clay typical of the period. One was obviously a perfume container. Its slender neck was chipped, and for half an hour I hunted through the rubbish pile to find the matching pieces. The other was an egg-shaped jug with a pointed base on which it stood when buried in the sand. The jug, probably a container for wine, was filled with tightly packed dirt; to protect it from further damage, I would wait until I returned to Jerusalem before emptying it.

Back in the village I showed my finds to sheik Aziz, but he was not impressed. It puzzled him that I should find two old jars to be of such value. But for me the jars were priceless, further establishing as they did the high civilization of the Canaanites and Hebrews who had lived in the Judean hills.

The sheik regretted that I must return to Jerusalem, but he was gratified to hear I would return one day with tools and equipment to excavate the temple area. He refused payment for his courtesy but accepted silver coins for the poor of his village. I could not leave his house before taking coffee. While it was served I asked Aziz if he knew why his village bore the name of Zorah.

"It has no special meaning," he replied. Dissatisfied with his answer, I explained that the name of every city, town, and village has a story behind it, and that this was true also of his own. I told him of the Biblical King Saul whose headquarters against the Philistines had been in a town reminiscent of his name. Now he understood, and told me this story remembered from his childhood:

"Many years ago there lived in these hills a man known for his extraordinary strength. He had the strength of ten men; with one hand he could lift a heavy plow. But he had a single flaw: he was too fond of women. As the years passed his strength grew smaller. This man spent much time in the house of a beautiful widow. But she did not love him; rather she feared him, for he was the enemy of the man she loved. One day the widow asked him what it was that made him so strong, and he answered laughingly: "My long curled hair." The next night, in his sleep, she cut his hair, and in the morning showed her true lover into the room. The strong man's strength was gone, and he was murdered like a helpless lamb."

"Who told you this story?" I asked the sheik.

"My grandfather, who heard it from his father before him. By Allah, I have not invented it."

Aziz' story was as important to me as the finding of the two Canaanite jars.

When I took the two jars from my knapsack back in Jerusalem, Sonja was at my side. Carefully I tapped out the dirt that filled the wine jug. A solid object caught my eye, then another. As I dusted them quickly my heart began to pound. They were two solid gold earrings, untarnished by the centuries — one in the shape of a bull's head, the other in the form of a coiled snake.

Gold objects from the early Hebraic period were very rare; only two or three similar pieces had ever been discovered. How had these found their way into the jar, and the jar into the priest's chamber? Perhaps some Hebrew or Philistine noblewoman had hidden them there as a safeguard against thieves. My first one-man expedition had brought results beyond my dreams.

Early the next morning I hurried through the city to the home of Flinders Petrie. He was pleased with the jars, and placed them in the first period of the Judges, around 1200 B.C.

"A good find," said Petrie, "You have done very well."

"There is something else," I said, and unwrapped the two gold earrings. The excitement and pleasure on Petrie's face was worth more to me than the earrings themselves. He called in Lady Petrie, and she asked the servant to bring wine for a celebration.

"What an auspicious beginning for your new career, Paul," said Lady Petrie.

"It was by the sheerest luck that I found the earrings," I told her. "I could easily have overlooked the jar they were in."

Lady Petrie regarded me with her serene gray eyes. "That would

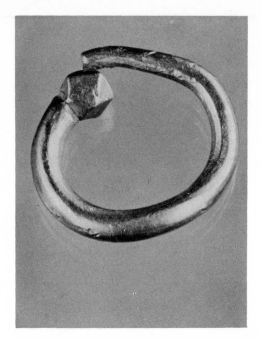

Two gold earrings, one in the shape of a bull's head 1¼″ long, the other in the shape of a coiled snake 1″ in diameter.

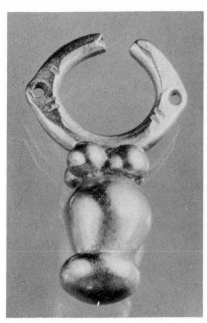

never have happened; the relics of the past have an irresistible magnetic power for those who search for the truth. Either they draw themselves to you, or you draw yourself to them. Don't call it luck, Paul — unless you also consider it luck that you chose archaeology as a career."

I realized what she meant, yet I have come to believe that, despite Lady Petrie, luck is the archaeologist's invisible assistant, and I have in fact included a group of stories elsewhere in this book to illustrate the point.

PART TWO

» V «

The Golden Locust

TRACING the origins of the Bible can be as exciting as a mystery thriller. In fact, the detective work that goes into many archaeological finds is not dissimilar to the byplay dreamed up by fiction writers. While there is certainly a great satisfaction in orderly research that progresses step by step to the successful excavation of a site, for spine-tingling thrills nothing can match the occasional excursions of a free-lance archaeologist into instinctive and deductive exploration.

In this chapter I have gathered together four different stories concerning important Biblical finds that resulted from more or less unorthodox archaeological detective work. The first one — the golden locust — is a rare treasure. In addition to being a magnificent work of art, it represents the first proof found by any archaeologist of the celebrated locust worship by pagan Philistine and Canaanite priests. Although idols of gold in insect form had been offered by the priests of Beelzebub to the gods of the insect world to prevail upon them to hold back the locust plagues, there was little knowledge of these strange rituals, the only references to them being in the Bible and in Thucydides.

It began — as these archaeological adventures often do — with a visit from an Arab friend to my house on Musrara Street. His name was Hassan, and he lived on the outskirts of Beth-shan with his two wives on a vegetable farm. He was a very poor man. I had not seen him since the days of Hamilton's and Iliffe's Beth-shan expedition, when, because his field was near our site, I had visited him frequently in search of antiquities. At the time I had told Hassan that should he find any objects of the past, he would be liberally rewarded for bringing them to me.

It would have been impolite for me to inquire immediately into the reason for his errand. My wife made coffee and I asked Hassan if he was hungry. He was not embarrassed to say he was. While the meal was served we spoke of everything and anything except the reasons for his presence in my house.

Hassan complained bitterly about his life and fate. He was unhappy with his sixty-odd years. His two wives, married some thirty years ago, and beyond the age of childbearing, were good only for work in the house and the fields. It did not look as though he would mount to Allah's heaven leaving an heir behind him. "My wives bore only daughters," he lamented. "Yet, all is not sadness. I am still hale and strong. The walk to Jerusalem took me only twelve days."

I was impressed; what he had come to say or to bring me must be very important indeed.

After dinner the old man bathed his tired feet in the bucket of luke-warm water my houseboy Mahmud had placed near his chair. When his feet were dried I knew it was time to begin our conversation. But still he seemed reluctant to speak. He glanced about the room as if to make sure we were really alone, and when Mahmud brought coffee, drank it in silence. Then, studying my face closely as if to reassure himself about my honesty and good intentions, he reached inside his robe and brought forth a small and soiled linen bag.

He dipped into the bag and took out a reddish-brown carnelian seal-stone, conical-shaped and about an inch and a half long. It bore an engraving of a priest before an altar, and had been used centuries ago to sign documents made of clay. The sealstone appeared to be early Assyrian in design. I dated it between 1000 and 900 B.C.

I was disappointed; the sealstone was definitely no rarity. Stones like it had been found not only in the Beth-shan area, but in many ruins of the early Babylonian and Assyrian eras. I had seen innumerable seal-stones in any number of museums. But Hassan would have been insulted had I told him this. I nodded over the stone admiringly for a moment and then as I was about to hand it back to him, something caught my eye. With my magnifying glass I saw on one side the engraving of a locust.

"Where did you find this?" I asked.

My question made him uneasy. "I cannot tell you," he muttered.

"It is important. I must know."

"You have the stone. I came especially to Jerusalem to bring it to you. I walked twelve days. Don't ask me any more questions."

I emptied my pocket of its silver coins and poured them into his hand.

"We are friends, brothers," I said. I assured him no one would know he had brought me the stone; that I was interested not in how he had acquired it, but where in the vicinity of Beth-shan. I spoke to him as to a child, and gradually his fears diminished as I resumed my questions. But I knew his answers were untrue.

"Hassan," I said sternly, "you are not telling the truth."

"If I do, it will go badly with me."

"Nothing will happen to you. I promise it."

He looked at me shrewdly. "You will swear by Allah?"

"I will swear," I assured him.

"Very well, *Chawadjah*." Hassan had, he told me, noticed a loose slab in the altar in the closely guarded Canaanite temple in Beth-shan. He had dislodged it with his knife, reached in, and discovered the seal-stone. When he heard a watchman approaching he had replaced the slab and escaped.

The site of Beth-shan is generally regarded as a Biblical historic shrine. I had among my papers several sketches I had made of the temple. The temple's outstanding features were its two-foot walls encircling the temple area, the remains of several chambers, and the seven weathered stone steps leading to a platform upon which the ruins of the altar stood. I showed my sketches to the old man.

"Yes," he said, pointing to the altar, "This is where I found the stone."

Hassan had committed theft, and unknowingly I had instigated it. Having helped many archaeologists excavate the Beth-shan area, he was intimately acquainted with it, and the basic methods of archaeology itself were no secret to him. For me he was a good man to know. He had proved that Canaanite altar stones were used as hiding places for priceless priestly objects, something up to that time unknown. But with the stone in my pocket I was as big a thief as he. The sealstone belonged to the government.

I was in a dilemma. The stone was too important a discovery for me to entrust to Hassan for its safe return, nor would my possessiveness allow me to yield it up to the Department of Antiquities. Finally I sent the old man away, assuring him I would be in touch with him again during the two days he planned to stay in Jerusalem.

There is mention in the Bible of the Philistines and Canaanites using idols of gold and silver (I Samuel 6: 4f.). After Hassan left, I couldn't get the locust out of my mind. The stone itself was proof of locust worship, but I knew I would never rest until I made certain that the compartment wasn't holding back anything from me.

The next morning I called on Dr. Iliffe at the Department of Antiquities. Iliffe was enthusiastic about my find, but doubted I would be able to find religious objects made of the precious metals of Beth-shan. I asked permission to do additional research, not excavation, within the fenced-in temple area. Iliffe was unable to make an immediate decision, but he promised to discuss the matter with the proper authorities and let me know their verdict as soon as possible.

When a week passed and I had heard nothing, I phoned Iliffe, only to find he had been called back unexpectedly to England. During the rush of departure he had undoubtedly forgotten my problem. I took the bus to Beth-shan for another talk with Hassan.

I drew a grasshopper on a piece of paper and told him I wanted him to return to the altar cache and look for any object he might find resembling what I had drawn.

He nodded. "I'll look for it as soon as I get an opportunity."

I was conspiring unlawfully to find an object which, if it existed, would be the property of Palestine's British Mandate government. I quieted my conscience with the thought that my purpose, after all, was a good one: to find confirmation of the Bible. Where strict ethics were concerned I should have waited for Iliffe's return, or taken up the question with Hamilton or my colleagues at the American School of Oriental Research. But I honestly believed the matter was a personal one — between myself and history. In any case, my impatience was too great to be contained.

I gave Hassan a pound note, promising him ten more if he returned to Jerusalem with what I hoped he would find. But when three weeks had passed with no sign of him, I gave up hope and attended to more pressing matters. My son, born the year before, had come down with diphtheria, and in the worry and anxiety Hassan left my mind.

In summer Jerusalem is like an open oven, and to escape the discomfort it was my habit to nap during the hottest part of the day. I was not the only one; from twelve to four Jerusalem was a deserted city. Mahmud knew that during the hours of siesta I was under no circumstances to be disturbed.

One afternoon about two months after I had last seen Hassan in Bethshan, I got up from my bed and went through the house to the servants' quarters.

"Any messages?" I asked Mahmud.

"None, sir. There was no one here, only an old Arab. I knew he would only be a nuisance, and I told him you were out of the city."

"What did he want?" I asked casually.

"I don't know. The man acted strangely. He would not leave his name. He only repeated over and over again a single word: *arbeh, arbeh. . . .*"

Arbeh meant locust. "Where did this man go?" I asked sharply. "Where can I find him?"

"I do not know, *Chawadjah*."

"Did he say he would be back?"

"I told him you were away."

I was angry, but managed to keep my temper; Mahmud had meant well enough. Dressing quickly, I hurried into the city in search of Hassan.

I knew nothing more about Hassan than his first name and that he lived in Beth-shan. Finding one particular Arab in Jerusalem was like looking for the proverbial needle. Was my best chance in the bazaars, the market places, the coffeehouses? I ran from place to place scanning the dark and curious faces, but saw no sign of him.

Could the old man have gone to say his prayers? I darted through the crowds to the Mosque of Omar, and stood there for two hours, watching the worshipers enter and depart. At nightfall I set on a round of the cheap hotels where for a few pennies visiting Arabs spent the night. In the Jerusalem summers patrons of the third-rate hotels sleep on mattresses lined in rows on the roof. I climbed the ancient stairways to the roofs and, moving from mattress to mattress, stared into the sleeping faces.

On the way home I searched the bazaars and coffeehouses again. It was after midnight when I let myself in the door. Suddenly a thought struck me: the antique dealers! Surely Hassan would not for a moment have hesitated to sell what he had brought me to a dealer known for his good prices. There were only four such dealers in antiquities in Jerusalem. Even if none of them recognized the locust's historical importance, all of them would know it was a rare object, worth a fortune to any of the museum's or collector's representatives who came from Europe and America just to buy such items. My imagination ran wild, and I saw the graven image glittering in Hassan's wrinkled palm as he offered it for sale.

The Golden Locust

I made the rounds of the dealers early the next morning. It would have been stupid for me to have inquired if an old Arab had offered them an object of priceless worth; I told them instead I was interested in an item I understood had been found recently in Beth-shan. Ohan, Jerusalem's outstanding Arab dealer, invited me to return later in the evening, saying he might have some information for me by then. If Ohan got hold of the locust it would be lost to me forever; I could never afford the price he would demand for it.

Wearily I toured the coffeehouses again, asking for Hassan. By late evening I had given up. Undoubtedly he had returned to his village. My one hope now was that the locust was still in his possession, not stolen or bought by a shrewd Arab middleman.

At that moment, passing by the police station in the Arab quarter, I decided to drop in on Inspector Khalil of the British police, an old acquaintance. I was lucky; Khalil was on duty, and asked immediately what he could do for me. Despite his youth — he was no more than thirty — Khalil was an important official. A man of almost three hundred pounds, he moved slowly, but mentally he had the agility of a weasel. Khalil had the reputation of being able to catch a thief before his theft was accomplished.

I told him my story. Khalil thought a moment; then he asked, "How old is this man?"

"Sixty, maybe seventy."

"How many wives has he?"

"Two, so far as I know."

"How old?"

I remembered having seen Hassan's wives in his courtyard. "Over fifty," I said, "at least. But what has this to do with it?"

Khalil laughed, his enormous belly shaking. "Oh, a great deal. And this Hassan, is he a poor man?"

"A pound note is a fortune to him. He walked the forty miles from Beth-shan to save the fare."

Stepping to the door, Khalil called a policeman. He whispered something to the man, then turned back to me. "Go with him," he said, smiling. "He will find your precious Arab."

Again I was in the narrow streets of the Arab section, by now as familiar to me as the back of my hand. We entered one of the coffee-houses where I had already been. I told my companion I had searched here, but he talked quietly to the proprietor, who led us through the main room, where Arabs sat over their coffee, to a small door at its back. We passed into a room filled with the sweet and pungent odor of hashish. As my eyes grew accustomed to the darkness, I saw about fifteen Arabs sprawled out on the floor. Their eyes wide open, they breathed heavily in sleep, lost in the green meadows of nirvana.

"Please, sir, look for your man," the policeman said.

Studying their faces, I examined the men one by one. In a corner I found Hassan. He was too deep in a hashish sleep to be aroused.

"Can he be moved?" I asked.

The policeman examined him briefly and shook his head. "He should remain undisturbed for at least another fifteen hours. To wake him now would harm him."

Where had Hassan gotten the money to buy hashish, I wondered. Had he sold the locust? I began to perspire.

"Underneath his *gallabiyya* (cloak)," I told the policeman, "there is a small leather pouch. There, I believe, is the object I am seeking. May I look for it?"

The policeman nodded.

Reaching inside Hassan's robes I found the pouch, fastened around his neck with a leather strap. I opened the pouch and anxiously explored it with my fingers. My face was close to Hassan's and his heavy breath was hot against my cheek. He groaned.

I touched something small and solid, and probing more deeply, closed my fingers around it. When I took it from the pouch, I saw in the dim light a golden locust of consummate workmanship. My calculations, then, had proved correct; near the sealstone Aziz had found a graven image.

Golden locust, 1⅜″ long.

I composed myself and rose to my feet. "I have what I want," I told the policeman.

In the main room of the coffeehouse I turned to the proprietor, "When this man awakes tell him *Chawadjah* Ilton was here and took what is his. Tell him to come to my house immediately." I gave the proprietor fifty *piasters*. "This will take care of what he owes you. Be sure he has a solid meal when he wakes up."

Outside I asked the policeman, "How did the Inspector know Hassan would be here?"

He smiled. "That was simple. For an old Arab, a poor man with two wrinkled wives, there is only one cheap pleasure left he can afford — hashish. In his dreams he may imagine he is a young man again, enjoying the pleasures of youth and women."

It was late afternoon when Hassan arrived at Musrara Street. He was dressed neatly and cleanly and his beard was trimmed. "You have the *arbeh?*" he asked anxiously. I showed it to him, and gave him his price with a little over. He was a happy man. Hassan was the same happy man when I visited him a year later in Beth-shan. The reason was, perhaps, the new, young, third wife in his courtyard.

When Iliffe returned from England I told him about the entire affair. I was prepared to part with the locust; rightfully it belonged to the government. But Iliffe's decision was in my favor. Without me he felt the locust would never have been discovered, since the Beth-shan excavations were closed to further digging. He suggested I lend the locust to Jerusalem's Archaeological Museum for a period of three months, after which time it would become my property.

A week later Iliffe, Ben-Dor, and I went to examine the secret altar cache at Beth-shan. The hiding-place was empty except for a number of pottery shards. The date of these was later set as from the time of the Prophet Samuel, in the last half of the eleventh century B.C. This was the time the golden locust had been made and worshiped.

Many photographs have since been taken of my golden *arbeh*, and it has received notice in several archaeological books and monographs dealing with the Biblical period. For six months it was on display in Israel's exhibition of the history of Biblical Israel at the Metropolitan Museum of Art in New York.

2

Next in this group is the magnificent necklace that may have belonged to one of Solomon's wives. It was discovered in Ain Shems and is of considerable historical importance as the only piece of jewelry ever unearthed from the period of Solomon.

Dr. Elihu Grant had asked me to join the Haverford expedition, about to conclude its fourth and final excavation of the ancient burial mound of Ain Shems. Ain Shems was on the northern slope of the Judean mountains, approximately thirty-five miles from Jerusalem. The Englishman Duncan Mackenzie had in 1912 done archaeology a signal service there, but for some technical reason his expedition had been unable to finish its work. The Haverford expedition had continued where Mackenzie left off, opening a large area in the central hill not far from the ruins of an eighteenth-century Greek Orthodox monastery. But, committing a breach of archaeological etiquette, the second Haverford expedition had dumped its debris upon that of Mackenzie, blocking the central canal in which I believed antiquities of Solomon's period could be found. Any further excavation would be difficult.

Ain Shems, called Beth-shemesh in the Bible, is often referred to there:

"And the cows went straight in the direction of Beth-shemesh along one highway, lowing as they went; they turned neither to the right nor to the left, and the lords of the Philistines went after them as far as the border of Beth-shemesh" (I Samuel 6:12, *RSV*).

"Now the people of Beth-shemesh were reaping their wheat harvest in the valley; and when they lifted up their eyes and saw the ark, they rejoiced to see it (I Samuel 6:13, *RSV*).

"The cart came into the field of Joshua of Beth-shemesh and stopped there. A great stone was there; and they split up the wood of the cart and offered the cows as burnt offering to the LORD" (I Samuel 6:14, *RSV*).

Although Ain Shems had at one time been an important town, neither Mackenzie nor the Haverford expedition had discovered any substantial evidence in confirmation of the Bible. Yet my own considerable research, done prior to joining the Haverford group, had convinced me that the Ain Shems region, meaningful for every student and reader of the Bible, should be prodigal in revealing secrets of the Biblical past.

The names of many Arab villages of the area indicated a close connection with Biblical history. All three names, Shemesh, Shems, and Samson are derivations of the word "sun." In ancient literature, especially among the Egyptians, the sun was the accepted synonym for "day" or "heavens." Samson's blindness, as recounted in the Biblical story, is symbolic of the end of his "day"; the blind cannot see the sun and blinded, Samson became powerless. Similar chronicles symbolizing day and night, sight and blindness are found in ancient Babylonian and Egyptian literature. I therefore came to the conclusion that Beth-shemesh had received its name from early Canaanite settlers whose culture and civilization were strongly influenced by the Egyptian or Babylonian religion.

This theory became the basis of my research. I was able to trace the existence of the hill of Ain Shems as an inhabited town back to 1800 B.C., when a small group of Canaanites had farmed the area. No remains of this early Canaanite period had been found, and the only written evidence of Canaanite settlement I discovered was in Egyptian hieroglyphic writing of the fifteenth century B.C., in which Beth-Shemesh was mentioned as an Egyptian military stronghold. This was in the time of the Hyksos, the Mesopotamian shepherd kings who conquered Egypt during the Hebrew patriarchal period. Later the town became Philistine, and subsequently fell under Hebrew domination in the time of Joshua, after the Exodus from Egypt. Beth-shemesh was later completely destroyed by the Babylonians around 587 B.C., when Nebuchadnezzar conquered Jerusalem.

Beth-shemesh, I was certain, had been important in the period of Solomon, about 950 B.C., when he had received the neighboring town, burned and gutted by a punitive Egyptian army, as dowry from the Pharaoh. The period of Solomon had been overlooked in previous research and excavation, and it was the one that interested me most.

Surprisingly, we know more about Beth-shemesh before 950 B.C. than we know about it in the time of Solomon. Between 1800 and 1200 B.C. it was a lively town, important in trade and commerce; and in the next two hundred years a heavily fortified one, for Mackenzie had given us proof that in the latter period the city was strongly walled. These city walls as well as the city itself must have been destroyed shortly before the time of Solomon, probably in the years when nearby Gezer was gutted by Egyptian armies. Even then the city was never completely uninhabited; ruins of small shops and houses have been found, many of them by the Palestine Exploration Fund. Duncan Mackenzie's book, *Beth-shemesh*, published by Haverford College, was extremely helpful in giving me this background information.

Though the Haverford expedition planned to dig only in the Byzantine level, less ancient than the period of Solomon by sixteen hundred years, I was glad to be a member of the party. Altogether the expedition spent ten days at Ain Shems, where it hoped to find outlying foundations of a Greek monastery going back to the eighth century A.D. In the vicinity of the monastery small chambers and floors were unearthed, but despite the fact that Byzantine stones and masonry had been used in their making, in general construction they were Arabic, from a period roughly a thousand years later than the Byzantine. Glassware, glazed pottery, and Arab ceramic as well as silver jewelry were found, but the expedition had met with no noteworthy success.

In Jerusalem I had long discussions with Hamilton, Flinders Petrie, and Sukenik, to whom I outlined my speculative theory that Ain Shems in the time of Solomon was the accepted Egyptian worshiping place in the Hebrew kingdom, and the only town in Judea-Canaan where Egyptian religious influence was still dominant.

Solomon in his devotion to Yahweh was a pious man. But he was also a tolerant one, and much more so than his fellow Hebrews. During his reign there were probably Egyptians in Jerusalem and a number of Solomon's wives, concubines, and officials may have been of Egyptian origin. Where could these people perform their strange, un-Hebrew rites of worship? Gezer was destroyed, but Beth-shemesh was still inhabited. Solomon must have permitted the Egyptians of Jerusalem to worship their gods outside the city, and such a place could only have been on the border of his kingdom closest to Jerusalem and in an area where Egyptian influence was still strong.

In the time of Solomon the Hebrew world was dominated by theology, and the Mosaic commandments were strongly adhered to:

> You shall have no other gods before me.
> You shall not make yourself a graven image.
> You shall not take the name of the LORD your God in vain.

In Beth-shemesh other gods were worshiped and graven images were erected to them, surely to the horror of all good Hebrews. To the Hebrews Beth-shemesh must have been ill-famed and despised and perhaps, it had occurred to me, this animosity had been carried down to the present day in the taboos and superstitions of the local Arabs.

The Arabs believed Ain Shems was haunted, and therefore taboo. No Arabs lived in Ain Shems itself and the fields of the area were uncultivated. I had spent some time conversing with the Arabs of the nearby village of Der Aban, and they had been reluctant to discuss the matter at all. During the Haverford expedition, fifteen Palestine policemen had stood guard against possible attacks from the fanatic villagers. Thirty years before, it was likely that threats from the natives had forced Mackenzie to leave the site.

I had heard no local legends to explain the Arabs' present attitude and several learned sheiks in Jerusalem could give me no answer to my question. Could the superstition, I wondered, have stemmed from the time of Solomon himself? Was there a link between the ancient Hebrew interdiction and the modern Arab taboo? These were at least tenable hypotheses.

I bore in mind that the Moslems living today in the villages of Palestine, Transjordan, Syria, and other countries of the Bible are descendants of the ancient Canaanites, Philistines, and Hebrews. During different periods of history these peoples were forced to change their religious beliefs, but they did not emigrate. In Palestine, after the destruction of the Temple by the Romans in A.D. 70, the Hebrew state ceased to exist. Conservative historians such as Gretz, Dubnow, and Elias Auerbach estimate that one million were killed in the fighting, nearly one million emigrated, and one million remained. These were the peasants and farmers, in general the village dwellers who could not afford to leave the country.

A vacuum of religious belief existed in the Holy Land. Some Hebrews followed Christ, others adhered to Roman paganism, others held to gnostic beliefs. When in the sixth century Palestine fell under Moslem domination many people became Moslems. These Moslems were descendants of the ancient Hebrews who did not flee the Holy Land after the decline and fall of the Hebrew state.

Since in Palestine the Canaanites were the ancestors of the Moslems, why should the Hebrew spiritual heritage not be part of their folklore? I had found enough story, legend, and saga among the primitive Arabs to link them to the Biblical past. In his features the Arab was strongly Semitic, and had a greater physical similarity to the people of the Bible than any other people of the world except the Jews of the Diaspora themselves. Even in the Arab's customs and traditions of today there was much evidence of their Biblical heritage.

Ever since I had lived in Palestine I had felt that a strong and natural brotherhood should exist between the Moslem Arabs and the Zionist Jews. Not only were they related as cousins through the patriarch Abraham, from whose sons Isaac and Ishmael their origin derived; their historic development through the centuries had been noticeably similar, if not the same.

With my friend Father Alexander, prior of the small monastery of El-Gamal that stood atop a mountain near Ain Shems, I went down into the village on my second trip to the area to ask questions of the people, the answers to which might explain their taboo. For nearly thirty years Father Alexander and his monks had conducted minor excavations in and around the monastery. They had unearthed early Arabic and Byzantine glassware, Roman vases, some interesting bronze implements of Etruscan origin, and a number of clay and pottery vases and statuettes dating back to the early and middle Iron Age. In the monastery was a special room where these relics were neatly labeled and exhibited in glass cupboards.

The Father and I had fair success with our inquiries. Some village elders spoke to us of Malak, a king who had once ruled here tyrannously; another Arab recalled that once in Ain Shems had stood a great statue of a pagan god who each night came to life to tempt and pursue the prophet Mohammed. We heard nothing of Solomon's reign, although some details of the taboo were made clearer to me.

He who broke the taboo of Ain Shems, we heard, would be tempted into evil; and he would also be cursed by sterility. Sterility for a Moslem was the greatest punishment imaginable, for children were not only proof of a man's virility and a good in themselves; they were a pledge that the Moslem belief in Allah would not die but continue through generations to come.

The same fear of punishment, I believed, must have existed three thousand years ago among the Hebrews. He who worshiped gods other than Yahweh would raise pagan children who would be lost to the Hebrew tribe, and therefore worthless. The survival of the tribe and the religion of Yahweh were of the first necessity to the small Hebrew nation. The stringency of the present-day Arab taboo convinced me that the original Hebrew interdiction of Solomon's time had been absorbed into Arab folklore and modified in accordance with it. If this was true, I should be able to find at Ain Shems concrete evidence in support of my theory.

In Jerusalem I received permission from the Department of Antiquities to examine finds made by all previous expeditions to Ain Shems, and I spent more than three weeks in the cellar of the Museum, making sketches of important pieces. Dr. Ben-Dor of the Museum staff was assigned to assist me. Most of the objects were clay and pottery dating from the period 1500 B.C. to A.D. 1000. There were, however, bronze implements from the middle and late Bronze periods; daggers, spearheads, bracelets, and rings; a length of chain that had probably been part of a horse's bit. One object of interest was a cartouche, the royal insigne, purported to be from the period of Tuth-moses III, the great Egyptian pharaoh who reigned from 1490 to 1436 B.C. There was a large nine-handled pot over two feet high with a rope molding at its base, and a massive oil container of double stone vats.

What fascinated me most were a fragment of a bronze-riveted tool and a small dipper jar still containing lumps of sulphur. These were from the time of Solomon and the early Hebrew kingdom, and the level in which they had been found would reveal what I was looking for.

I wondered why no jewelry had been found in previous Ain Shems excavations. In none of the archaeological records have I found evidence of Ain Shems' having been ransacked by grave robbers, and history made no mention of invaders looting or pillaging the town. The excavations had shown clearly that no natural catastrophes had later occurred. These facts and the central fact that no jewelry had yet been found from the time of Solomon made me feel certain that excavators of the second level had far from exhausted its potentialities.

This, then, was the method of my research. First I examined the particular site, taking into account the results of all previous excavations, including their records and discoveries; second, I analyzed folklore and superstition relating to the site or area, and tried to winnow from it those truths or half-truths which, with the help of deduction, led me to a direction or a conclusion, and allowed me to reconstruct with fair accuracy events that occurred thousands of years in the past.

It was six months before I could return to Ain Shems. The discovery of the golden locust had proved the validity of my lone-wolf methods, and I had greater confidence both in these and in what my Jerusalem colleagues referred to as my unorthodox intuition. Since Zorah I had gone on no expedition. I applied for the necessary authorization and was ready to leave.

I was convinced my research into the period of Solomon was basically correct. Besides luck, I felt that all I needed to prove my theory that in Solomon's time Ain Shems was an accepted place of foreign worship in the Hebrew Kingdom was the evidence discoverable only in the ruins themselves.

But despite my confidence I tried to keep a sense of balance. I was fully prepared for failure. My first unlucky lesson in unrestrained enthusiasm had taken place not far from Jerusalem in a small village near the Jordanian border. That day, seeing a woman of sixty working alone in the fields, I asked her if she had ever come across an object strange or unknown. Often in this part of the world, I told her, the *fellahin* found articles while plowing, among them old pots, small figurines, and even bronze or bone implements.

The woman nodded; once she had found such an article. Unable to describe it, she could only tell me it was worthy of a king alone. I could not hide my excitement and curiosity and demanded that she bring me to her prize.

For nearly two hours I waited impatiently while she finished her work in the fields. At sunset she took me to the village, where I waited in her courtyard. She came out carrying a little bundle of cloth. Carefully she unwrapped one piece of material, then another and still another. Her treasure stood revealed. It was an unusual find for an Arab peasant woman, even one who lived in the twentieth century. For the piece was nothing other than a broken electric plug, most likely tossed out of a passing car. "I found it long ago," she said, "and I knew one day I would exchange it for a fortune in gold."

I did not have the heart to tell the old woman her electric plug would be without historical value until the year 5000. In consolation I gave her a silver coin, but assuming this was my offer of payment, she shook her head. Smiling, I told her that one day perhaps a man would give her gold. "I am not rich enough," I said, "to buy this from you."

In my own experience, out of a hundred excavations only fifteen to twenty have been rewarding. Often my archaeological calculations would be correct, the modern geographic location corresponding perfectly with the ancient site, the historic research irreproachable. All indications pointing to the presence of an ancient tomb, ruin, or city wall, I would hire Arab workers, buy picks and shovels, fence off the area, and start to dig.

The first day, no results. The second, only earth and sand. And the same for days and days until both my money and patience were exhausted. I have had to cease work ignominiously, and return empty-handed to whatever town or city was then my Middle-Eastern headquarters. Yet two years later, another expedition would dig ten yards from my excavation, and discover the site of a forgotten civilization or culture.

Another time I heard of an ancient Greek silver figurine rumored to have been found near Ashkelon in the south of Palestine. I knew the Arab fisherman said to have discovered it while excavating for the foundations of his new house and made the long trip to see him, only to learn that the figurine had been bought by an Englishman from Jerusalem the day before. Weeks later I saw the impressive ten-inch figurine in Dr. Hamilton's study in the Rockefeller Museum. Hamilton had acted faster upon the information than I had. But such failures, personally crushing though they may be, are unlikely to interest the reader, and a recital of them has been eliminated from this book.

I knew that my understanding of the Arab mentality would be of great help in the Ain Shems project. It was impossible to predict how much trouble the local Arabs might cause, but I was certain that the famous taboos would enter into the picture somewhere.

The gap between the modern educated Westerner and the Arab Moslem is deep and sometimes unbridgeable. It is not enough for the Westerner to understand the Arab's way of life, his traditions, his religion. You must tune your heartbeat to his own. The Arab peasant is emotional and closed to reasonable argument. He is either friend or foe. The nuances in between, common in the Western world, are unknown to him.

In the Middle East, therefore, each new acquaintance is a new and demanding experience. Whenever I came into a new village and met new people, it was necessary to use all the psychology at my command. Even when I returned to a village where I had reason to believe I had made friends already, I was often obliged to renew friendships all over again.

For the Arab *fellah* mistrusts the Westerner; to him every non-Moslem represents a world unknown. The reasons are not difficult to understand. The Arab, so far as the standards of the non-Moslem world are concerned, is completely uneducated. Centered in his present, with no comprehension of the past, he lives narrowly within the borders of his own culture and civilization. All events that happened before his own father was born are to him legend and saga. His life is anchored in his religious beliefs; Allah is his personal god and his relationship with Him is quite unique. He who does not believe in Allah is an unbeliever and inferior.

I have always carefully avoided theological discussion with the primitive Arab, and been reluctant to mention the word "Allah" in his presence. But when I found that the word "heart" is equivalent to the word "God" and can be substituted for it, I had discovered the psychological bridge to many of my Arab friends.

I planned to make my preliminary observations at Ain Shems alone, if possible unseen by the villagers. Only if I found sufficient evidence during this preliminary investigation would I start to excavate. The train trip from Jerusalem was a short one; past Bittir, a small Arab village near the ruins of the Maccabean fortress of Betar; past Der el-Sheik to the little village of Artuf, where we arrived before eight in the morning. From Artuf I hiked to the ruins of Ain Shems, food and a tea-filled thermos packed next to the tools in my knapsack.

The climb before me to the top of the hill plateau and the ruins was at least twelve hundred feet. The morning was fresh, the sky blue and cloudless. In the fields around me cornstalks ready for harvest trembled in the breeze. A ten-minute walk through the cornfields brought me to the slope of the hill, and I soon found a donkey path leading up the hill.

With my every step closer to the ruins I felt more certain of a success. The time passed quickly; as I climbed the sun was bright but not oppressive. There was a light, faintly cooling breeze. I felt no fatigue, though by this time I had already covered a good half of the way.

I climbed over the ancient rocks and walls to the site excavated by Duncan Mackenzie and began to tap the walls for an opening. Several hours later, with no success, I returned to Artuf, where I was the guest of an Arab landowner. My friends were pleased to see me; I brought them greetings from their son, a student in Jerusalem who was often my house guest. During our evening meal of *muchalabia,* a thick and viscous spinach soup, and *falafel* (baked vegetables), I learned that my host was unable to provide me with the help necessary for excavation. Moslems, fearing the Ain Shems taboo, refused to set foot upon the cursed ground.

At the site the next morning I sat down for a moment before beginning work alone. In that moment I felt far removed from the realities of contemporary life, and the present became one with the past in a curious manner that only the archaeologist knows, he who lives as much in one as the other.

Here and there inquisitive chameleons crept from the wall fissures to observe me. Insects filled the air. I remember trying to reconstruct in my imagination all that I had read about ancient Beth-shemesh.

I created in my mind the busy market place, the narrow streets, the inn, the temples. The men, their beards curled and ornamented with precious stones that glittered in the sunlight, bartered, argued, discussed. Like people of today both resentful and approving, they talked of mundane things: politics, the cost of living, the last address of King Solomon to the people of Jerusalem. They were apprehensive of the Philistine lord's secret enlargement of his army. They had news from Thebes of the Egyptian priests of Ptah who had developed a new ointment for mummification.

The women of Beth-shemesh wore transparent robes and heavy gold earrings, some in the shape of pyramids, some shaped like lotus flowers, dangled from their earlobes. Precious stones — emeralds, jaspers, carnelians, garnets — decorated their arms and ankles. The Egyptian priestesses wore about their thighs heavy gold bands engraved with the face of the goddess Isis.

In the middle of the market place was a well where slave women came to fill their pottery vessels with water that they carried back to the houses in the narrow streets. Near the wells sat a beggar, his bowl half filled with housewives' leftovers. From the temple came the chanting voices of the priestesses, hymning thanks to Amen, Isis, and Osiris. Worshipers went up and down the wide steps of the temple and townspeople passed in and out of the bathhouses on the other side of the square.

Through the columns I could see huge clay basins in which men and women stood naked while Nubian slaves emptied ewers of water over their heads. Musicians marched between the basins playing the lute, the sistrum, the cymbals, and the flute. Their tunes were popular, melodious; not monotonous like the temple chants. On low stone benches before the inn sat people drinking sweet heavy wine made from the grapes of Cyprus, Crete, and Lesbos.

Slowly I returned to the present, the vivid pictures of the past fading like a dream. It was time for work.

I took my tools from my knapsack: a small pick, a shovel, a hammer, sieve, my flashlight, and a magnifying glass. As I began to dig my way through the ruins of what I believed was the Egyptian stratum, I heard a sudden noise. It was not the hissing of a snake nor the rustling of a jackal or a fox. What I heard was the heavy breathing of a man. I turned my head and saw a very old man standing near me behind the wall.

No peasant or villager would have dared to approach the tabooed ruin. For a moment I thought the *fellahin* were right, that the place was haunted. Then I saw the old man smile, and he asked if I would accept him as a helper.

"I know the place well," he said. "Once I helped a learned man who asked that I shovel for him. That was long ago." He showed me the muscles of his arms and legs. "I'm still strong, *Chawadjah.*"

"But aren't you afraid of the devil?"

"*Chawadjah,*" the old man said, "I'm eighty-five years old. I have had five wives; I have thirty children and grandchildren. I am afraid of nothing."

I laughed and shook his hand, glad that he was joining me.

Despite his age, Ibrahim was strong as a mule. The heavy stone blocks he carried might have been pebbles, for all the effort they required of him. Soon we began shoveling the ground away. I had no assurance I had hit upon the right spot for excavation; I knew only that here the heavy preliminary work had been done decades ago by Mackenzie. Ibrahim and I worked steadily at removing the hardened earth at least six feet below the general level of the ruins. After two hours of concentrated labor we struck rock again.

"*Chawadjah,* this is the wrong place," said Ibrahim.

Reluctantly, I agreed. We covered over the large hole we had dug and rested for half an hour before choosing a new spot several feet away. Once again we marked off an area and started to excavate through the various layers. And once again we hit solid rock. Ibrahim seemed discouraged and ready to call it a day. But, unconvinced this time, I began carefully to remove earth from around the rock that barred our way. I soon discovered that this was no rock but a symmetrical stone two and a half feet in length. It appeared to be the first of several steps leading below. I was certain I had discovered the entrance-way leading either to a single tomb or to a grave chamber.

Ten minutes later the second step was cleared. I knew now this was a staircase. By comparing my level of excavation with the digging done previously by Mackenzie, I knew that any discovery I might make would definitely date from the time of Solomon.

We were now eight feet below ground level and had cleared seven steps altogether when a stone wall blocked our path. We began to remove earth from the bottom, sides, and top of this wall, which I knew had been placed there to close the entrance of a chamber. The next few minutes should tell the tale. If this were an Egyptian tomb, then there would be an ancient seal closing the grave hermetically from the outside. The steps and plate were both definitely Egyptian.

I was unable to find the seal or its remains. My next step would be to remove the stone plate, but our combined strengths could not budge it. I returned to ground level and suggested that Ibrahim come with me, but he started to work with my hammer. It seemed like a waste of time to me, as I listened to the old man hammering away below me, but he ignored my shouts to stop. It was obvious that we needed stronger tools and a heavy iron bar to use as a lever. Then, as I was gathering together our equipment for the trip back to the village, I heard a shout, *"Chawadjah,* the big stone moves!"* I quickly rejoined Ibrahim, and together we began to move the stone. Surprisingly, it was not fastened to the side walls with mortar, as it should have been. This meant either that the chamber was no tomb or that, if it was indeed a tomb, grave robbers had rifled it thousands of years ago, and destroyed the seal. Both possibilities were disappointing, and my enthusiasm waned. But when we had lifted the stone some three or four inches I noticed chisel marks. I cleaned them immediately, and saw they were hieroglyphics. One hieroglyphic remnant stood for a walled city, another represented the sun, which was also the sign for Isis, and a third was the hieroglyph of death. This was indeed a tomb, if a rifled one.

Ibrahim inserted two stones in the small opening to hold the plate fixed, and adding more stones to the opening, we lifted the plate inch by inch. After two hours of work the opening was large enough for me to poke in my flashlight. Cold, dank air escaped from the chamber, and in the flashlight's beam I saw a skull and scattered human bones. On the wall were more faint hieroglyphic signs: on one the sign of an *ankh* (♀), and on the other the knot *tedh* (∞), the symbol for death. Both were typical of Egyptian burial paintings. There were no urns or other pottery or marble containers.

An hour later the tomb opening was enlarged enough for me to crawl inside. Since there were no other hieroglyphic writings on the walls, I could not determine what rank of man or woman was entombed here. With my flashlight I examined the ground inch by inch, hoping to find at least some remnants of the burial gifts, or a piece of jewelry or a necklace bead. But the tomb had been ransacked with the painstaking care of professional thieves. I had been no more fortunate at Ain Shems than my colleagues.

I was about to leave the tomb when Ibrahim, stationed outside, whispered sharply, "Listen . . . listen!"

I heard what seemed to be the flapping of large wings.

"The devil, the devil!" Ibrahim whispered frantically. "Let me come in!"

"There is no devil," I replied. "What you hear is only the birds flapping their wings; they have nests in these ruins."

But now I heard the murmur of voices, and as I squatted in the opening of the tomb they became louder. These were the voices of men, and men were more dangerous than the devil! I began to crawl from the tomb.

The flashlight slipped from my hand, and its beam outlined something on the ground. I picked up the object, an alabaster container filled with earth. Hurriedly, I shook the dirt from the jar and several earth-encrusted objects tumbled into my hand. I shoved the jar and the pieces into my pocket and left the tomb. At the top of the steps stood Ibrahim, shaking and cowering.

For a moment the daylight blinded my eyes, and then I saw, standing fifteen yards away, at least thirty Arab *fellahin,* daggers in their hands.

We were in great danger. I had to think fast, and approaching the Arabs slowly, I held my hands empty before me to show I carried no weapon. I spoke to the hostile men in their native tongue, and told them I had come here to unearth from the ruins of Ain Shems the past of their own ancestors. I described the life that had been lived here thousands of years ago. And I began to tell them the story of Solomon.

God must have been with me, for the sheik ordered his men to sheathe their weapons. The distrust and anger left their faces, and they crowded around to listen. When I finished, darkness had fallen over the mountains of Judea and we were friends.

They were with me constantly and I had no opportunity to examine my find.

Back in the village, the sheik offered me lodging, but I refused and his men accompanied me to the little railway station of Artuf, where the sheik presented me with a basket of fruits grown in the mountains. I boarded the train to Jerusalem.

When the train was under way I took the jar and the almost unrecognizable objects from my pocket. Certainly of Solomon's period, the jar was typical of the art work exported by the Egyptians to the countries of the ancient world. But it was by no means proof that the temple at Ain Shems had been the worshiping place of the pagan foreigners at Solomon's court. Jars like it had been found in Egypt, Crete, and Cyprus.

Back in my Jerusalem study I began to clean the jar and remove the earth from around the pieces. After only a superficial layer of dirt had been removed, the pieces were revealed as the broken remnants of a glittering golden necklace. Only a small section about three inches long and containing an emerald was intact; the rest, consisting of gold beads in the shapes of bull heads and columns, beads of blue glaceed faïence, and two hammered gold lotus leaves, were scattered in the dirt.

When roughly assembled on my desk the necklace stood revealed as a piece of magnificent jewelry. I could hardly believe the dirt-packed jar had contained such loveliness. I examined the gold beads with a mag-

Golden necklace, 22″ long.

Center pendant 2″ long.

nifying glass. Each was a masterpiece of the ancient goldsmith's art. A layer of silvery patina covered the emerald, and the lotus leaves had been detailed with naturalistic perfection.

No poor and simple woman could have owned it: only a noblewoman close to the throne who had been buried in Beth-shemesh in great pomp and luxury. In the Cairo Museum I had seen similar gold jewelry of Egyptian origin found in the grave chambers of princesses and wives of Pharaohs. The necklace from Ain Shems was equally costly, equally beautiful. This necklace had possibly belonged to one of Solomon's Egyptian wives.

For many days visitors came to see it. My pride in the necklace, I thought, was justifiable. Not only was it unique as the only piece of jewelry of Solomon's time, but it was material proof of the Bible's description of Solomon's splendor and of his legendary gold from the land of Ophir: "And they went to Ophir, and brought from there gold, to the amount of four hundred and twenty talents; and they brought it to King Solomon" (I Kings 9:28, *RSV*). "Thus King Solomon excelled all the kings of the earth in riches" (I Kings 10:23, *RSV*).

3

Not far from some fortification ruins on Mount Zion is the Dominican church Domitio, where my friend Father Andreas was curator of the Museum. Domitio is built on the spot where, according to Biblical legend, Mary fell asleep and was carried to heaven. Hence the name Domitio, from *dormire*, the Latin verb for "sleep." Some ten yards from the church is the Arab-Christian quarter. Nearer the ruins are the small clay houses or primitively built huts of the very poor Moslems.

One day, strolling in the ruins and viewing Jerusalem below, I was joined by a small Arab boy from one of the nearby huts. Perhaps ten years old, the boy was bright and clever and an amusing talker. He searched in the pocket of his *gallabiyya* and brought forth an ancient silver coin, saying he had found it not five feet from the ruined walls.

I identified the coin as from the time of Alexander the Great, and exchanged it for modern Palestinian currency of larger denomination. I asked the boy, whose name was Adnam, if this was the first time he had found such a relic of the past.

He nodded. "But my elder sister Imre found something here among the rubbish some weeks ago."

"Perhaps I may see it?"

"I'll find my sister."

"Your sister doesn't live with you and your parents?"

"Yes, but during the day Imre works in the house of an Englishman."

"What is this man's name?" I asked, curious.

"I don't know. He works in the Museum."

I went through the names of my friends attached to the Rockefeller Museum. When I mentioned Hamilton, the boy nodded.

"That's it — *Chawadjah* Hamilton."

I smiled; I had seen Adnam's sister often at Hamilton's house, opening the door to visitors or serving refreshments to Mrs. Hamilton's guests. I felt it was probable that had Imre ever found anything of archaeological interest she would have offered it to her employer, who would have placed it among his collection or sent it along to the Museum.

A few days later I came to tea at the Hamiltons'. As always, Imre opened the door.

"I met your little brother Adnam," I said.

"He told me, *Chawadjah*," the girl said. "Adnam told me you gave him much money."

I would have liked to have spoken longer with Imre, but at that moment Mrs. Hamilton came into the hall. It would have looked highly suspicious had I continued with our conversation; as it was, my hostess' eyebrows rose slightly. In the Middle East one does not converse with Arab servants.

While we sipped our tea I turned the discussion to Mount Zion and the ruins. Hamilton was either noncommittal or disinterested in the topic of conversation, and I followed his wife's lead into another subject — domestics. I soon found out that neither of the Hamiltons had the slightest idea that Imre lived on Mt. Zion, near the ancient Biblical ruins. Later other guests joined us and I left after a pleasant evening. Most of all, I was pleased to have learned that Imre had no archaeological "connections" with her employers.

I could have seen Adnam again after school, but most of the late afternoons I was busy. Next Sunday I found Adnam and asked if he had talked with his sister. Not only had he talked with Imre; he showed me the object she had found. Round and hard, it was overlaid by a crust of thick, hard earth. I was unable to determine its exact shape and identity, although its weight indicated metal. Carefully scratching the exterior I saw that my first hunch was right; the object was made of bronze.

I asked Adnam if I could take the piece home to be cleaned in my study.

"Of course, *Chawadjah*," he said, "but I promised my sister you would pay her well." His eyes twinkled at me shrewdly.

"How much?" I asked.

Even Arab children are aggressive businessmen. He had seen my interest and the price had gone up. When he had named an exorbitant amount, I returned the object to him. "Adnam, I am sure ten *piasters* is a very good price, and that Imre would be delighted with it."

We settled finally at fifteen *piasters*, and my promise that if Imre could show me the exact spot where the object had been found, I would willingly pay her another two shillings. The deal was made, and in friendship we parted. At home, afraid of damaging the piece with a knife, I left it to soak overnight in water, expecting the earth to soften and be separated from the bronze.

In the morning there lay at the bottom of the glass container a perfect specimen of a bronze cymbal, typical of those used as musical accompaniment by musicians and priests for psalm-singing in the time of the great Hebrew kings. After drying and cleaning it, I saw that the small metal disc was covered with the green patina of bronze at least three thousand years old. This indeed was a significant find; and since cymbals always came in pairs, I might discover the cymbal's matching mate if Imre were able to show me where she had found it.

I went back to the ruins in search of Adnam the next day. But there was no sign of him. His father's hut was closed; perhaps the entire family had gone to the market place. I could not, of course, phone Mrs. Hamilton and ask about her maid. Patiently I waited near the house, sitting on the ruins of a wall. Patience is one virtue the archaeologist must have in long supply, as Flinders Petrie had often told me, and in my own life I have found it to be not only good professional but good general advice.

For three days I went daily in the afternoons to the little house on the Mount of Zion, but there was no trace of the boy, and the hut was always locked and closed. Sunday afternoon I tried my luck again, and this time I found him.

"Where have you been?" I asked.

He grinned. *"Chawadjah,* Imre and I decided to give the money you gave us to our father. We spent four fine days in the house of my aunt in Beth Jalla. I ate much *barrat* (ices) and *gelat (halvah)*; and there was dancing at the amusement park. The money was enough for the bus fare of my father, mother, and both my brothers."

"You can make a still longer visit to your aunt, if you have spoken well with your sister. Did Imre tell you where she found the object?"

Adnam said gravely, "She told me to say that if you will come tomorrow she will show you herself."

"How can Imre manage to get away from her work?"

The boy grinned widely. "If you pay her ten *piasters,* she will tell the English Madam she is ill and must go home."

"Agreed," I said, a little guiltily.

The next afternoon both Adnam and Imre were waiting for me at the ruins. Imre pointed to a crevice in the ruins not far from where I was accustomed to sit overlooking the Jerusalem view, and disappeared inside, motioning me to follow after her. I was less thin and agile than she, but somehow I managed, with Adnam behind me.

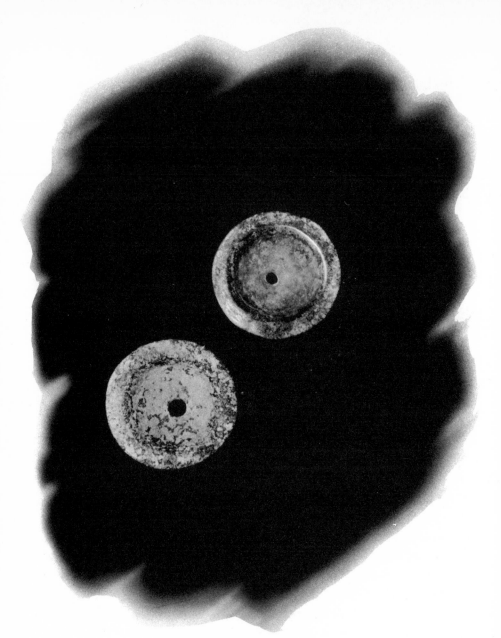

Bronze cymbals, 2¼" in diameter.

Imre led us past the crumbled ruins of an ancient wall to an open place. She pointed to a segment of wall of which there were several lower stones missing. "Here," she said, "on the ground in this space is where I found it."

"*Chawadjah*," said Adnam, "will you not give us our money now?"

"This is the place, I swear by Allah," said Imre, and held out her hand.

I examined the open space for a crevice, but there was none, and the earth was too hard for digging without a sharp shovel. Disappointed, I gave the girl her ten *piasters* and left the ruins.

I was sure Imre was telling the truth. Perhaps the cymbal's mate had been thrown away in the rubbish of the last excavation, some forty years before. As the weeks passed I was busy with other work, and the cymbal left my mind. But its mate that sat on my shelf was clearly marked, "Unfinished Business."

With the coming of winter Jerusalem had torrential rains. I spent the rainy season in Egypt and Europe, and when I returned it was February, and spring in the Holy Land. Again, after a hard day's work, I went to rest by the ruins, and remembering my unfinished business, I brought a garden trowel with me.

The rains had softened the earth, and digging near the oblong stone, my trowel struck something hard. It was the mate to my cymbal, covered by a hard crust of earth but immediately recognizable.

Home in my study I cleaned it and set it beside the other on my shelf. I was now the proud possessor of a pair of cymbals possibly used in the time of David, when the great King sang his songs in praise of God: "And David and all the house of Israel were making merry before the Lord with all their might, with songs and lyres and harps and tambourines and castanets and cymbals" (II Samuel 6:5, *RSV*). "The singers . . . were to sound bronze cymbals" (I Chronicles 15:19, *RSV*).

That evening I dropped in on Dr. and Mrs. Hamilton, bearing, more than a little guiltily, a huge box of candy. Mrs. Hamilton looked at my gift with surprise, but accepted it with pleasure. Later, leaving the house, I pressed ten *piasters* into Imre's hand. This gift was accepted with an impassive face, a surreptitious bow, and complete understanding.

4

Ben-Dor's message was urgent; I must come immediately to the Museum. It must be an important matter indeed, I thought, leaving the house; Ben-Dor knew I was busy with a forthcoming expedition to the Sinai Peninsula with Flinders Petrie.

As I entered his study, I could see that Ben-Dor was literally bursting with some extraordinary news. "All right," I said, "I'm waiting. What's the great discovery this time?"

He smiled. "How do you know we've made a great discovery?"

"Very simple. The key to the safe in your right hand."

Ben-Dor shrugged and, going to the wall safe, returned with a cardboard box. He opened it slowly and lifted from the cotton batting a small hand-carved wood figurine of an Egyptian house servant. Such figurines were placed in Egyptian solar boats, the symbolic boats of the dead buried with members of the Egyptian nobility and outstanding public personages. The Egyptians believed the solar boat guaranteed the dead smooth sailing into the afterworld, and that the wooden effigies of servants would come alive to resume their service in the hereafter.

I had seen many such solar boats in Cairo's Egyptian Museum and in the shops of antique dealers, and Ben-Dor's enthusiasm was difficult to comprehend. The figurine in itself was not an outstanding example of the woodcarver's art; the coloring was primitive and the carving crude, without the delicacy of other pieces like it made in the eighteenth and nineteenth dynasties (approximately 1500-1200 B.C.).

I returned the figurine. "Nice," I said, "but nothing special."

It was evidently the answer he had expected. I sat silently, waiting for him to continue. Ben-Dor was too considerable a scholar to call me across the city to see a routine wood carving of no great significance.

"I know," he began, "that in itself this figurine is unimportant. There are many others like it. Its distinction lies in the fact that it was found not in Egypt, but in Palestine."

I was properly amazed. Of course there had been, at various periods of ancient history, Egyptian penetration into Palestine. The Bible mentions Egyptian political influence in various provinces of Canaan from the time of the patriarchs (approximately 1800 B.C.) to the Exodus (approximately 1250 B.C.). Three hundred years after the Hebrew invasion of Canaan by Moses, Egypt occupied Canaan and built there a network of fortresses. But Egyptian tombs and burial objects had yet to be discovered in the soil of the Holy Land.

"Now you can understand my excitement," Ben-Dor said.

Indeed I could. "But how can you be sure this was found here?" I asked. "Did you discover it yourself?"

"No, but the Arab who ploughed it up is completely reliable."

"I wonder. Maybe it was given to him by an Egyptian relative or friend, and he lied about its place of discovery to get your price."

Ben-Dor shook his head decisively. "We made our own investigation. I can say with complete authority that this figurine was excavated in the soil of Palestine." Ben-Dor was known for his scholarly accuracy; I extended my hand and offered him my congratulations.

I took up the figurine and examined it more carefully. "Where was it found?" I asked in what I hoped was a casual tone of voice.

Ben-Dor shook his finger at me. "For the time being that is our secret. We don't plan to publish the find at the moment; nor will we exhibit it. In the near future we plan an excavation of the site where the figurine was found."

I took out my magnifying glass, hoping to detect its place of origin, and for the first time noticed remnants of gray-green soil in the deeper impressions the carver's knife had made. Ben-Dor clucked his disapproval and took back the figurine. He noted my smile anxiously. "Paul," he said with suspicion, "you're up to something."

"Not at all," I said, and thanking him, said good-by.

Back in my study I took up my work, but found it difficult to concentrate. Later that afternoon I dropped in on Adolf Reifenberg. I asked him if there was any area of Palestine that had soil of a peculiarly grayish-green tint. He told me there were several areas, off-handedly mentioning two of them in particular whose sulphur content produced this color. One of these areas was in the Jordan region, not far from the place where John the Baptist had baptized his followers from Judea. This area, however, I had to eliminate immediately; historic evidence showed that Egyptians had never settled or occupied military installations there. Another area, South of Gaza in the Negev, was more promising. Here, I felt, a peasant at his plow might well have turned up the wooden figurine. Before Gaza became a Philistine town it had been occupied on and off by invading Egyptian armies. These invasions had been referred to in the Tell el-Amarna tablets, as well as in other hieroglyphic writings on slabstones and columns in Edfu and other ruins discovered in upper Egypt. The crudity of Ben-Dor's figurine seemed to point to one of the earlier dynasties, the sixteenth or fifteenth B.C., when Egyptian armies had invaded Canaan and Joseph had been purchased from his brethren by merchants traveling the caravan route between Canaan and Egypt.

The figurine with its greenish soil haunted me. Should I be able to determine its place of discovery, I stood a good chance of finding additional objects that would shed light upon the period of the patriarch Jacob, his son Joseph, and the Hyksos shepherd kings.

The next day I took the bus to Gaza. The mayor of Gaza was one of my Arab acquaintances and would, I thought, help me in any way he could. But when I asked if he knew of any new discoveries in the area he shook his head. I knew that there was a relationship between sulphur content and soil fertility so I asked him where, south of Gaza, the best oranges grew. The best citrus fruit in Palestine was grown in the Gaza area, and certainly within the area there must be strips that yielded a better crop than others. The mayor told me the spot I was looking for was not far from Khan Junis, where several hundred acres produced superlative fruit. Khan Junis was only fifteen miles south of Gaza, and I took the bus that left the next hour.

Khan Junis was a large village with a single thoroughfare and farm-houses scattered to the left and right of it over a considerable distance. The village had a single coffeehouse where, typical of the Middle East, men relaxed under the palm leaves. Here I began my investigation. I asked the proprietor if he knew of an Arab farmer who had recently sold an archaeological object in Jerusalem for a good price. He had heard nothing of this and advised me to see the *muktar*, to whom I repeated my story. The *muktar*, a shifty-eyed middle-aged man, also said he knew of no such farmer, and told me that had the object been found in his district it would have fallen under his jurisdiction. He confirmed the high quality of Khan Junis' citrus fruit, and directed me to the spot where the best oranges grew.

I spent three hours examining the green-tinted soil of the premier strips, but found nothing. None of the dozen *fellahin* I spoke to knew anything of the wooden figurine. I knew my hunch was right, and that the figurine had come from this vicinity; the soil I had been sifting through was of the same color and consistency as that which had adhered to the servant figurine. But I would have to examine at least ten square miles of dirt, and this was clearly impracticable. I returned to the coffee-house, dined lightly, and waited for the bus for Gaza.

It was unbearable in the early afternoon heat, and my shirt was soaked with perspiration; never had I waited so eagerly for the sun to go down. There was an hour's wait for the Gaza bus, and I spent it pouring cold lemonade down my throat until it threatened to come out of my ears. The bus finally rattled to a stop in front of the coffeehouse, and I was depressed to see it was packed to capacity. Planned for twenty-four, it held at least forty, and I was lucky to squeeze myself in. Hot, disheveled, and miserable, I peered out upon the fields as we went. We had gone about five miles when the bus, already rattling alarmingly, broke down and stopped in the middle of the road.

Stoically, without complaint, the passengers filed out to take the air while the driver repaired his engine. When I asked him how long it would be before we were under way again, the driver, bent irritably over his carburetor, merely shrugged.

Attracted by our disaster, two little Arab girls had come from a nearby group of three or four clay huts to examine the passengers in the wide-eyed wonderment of children everywhere. One held a small doll in her hands, and unless I was dreaming, it was remarkably similar to the one I had seen in Ben-Dor's study. "Child, where did you get this?" I asked in rapid Arabic.

The little girl shrank back, and when I reached for the doll, ran frightened over the fields to one of the small clay huts. I reached the hut to find her sobbing in the doorway against the skirts of her mother.

I caught my breath and explained to the woman, who took the doll from the child and showed it to me. Similar in every respect to Ben-Dor's figurine, it had the same crude workmanship, the same coloring, the same details. Undoubtedly it had been carved by the same artist, and what I held in my hand was another figurine that had decorated the Egyptian solar boat upon which Ben-Dor's wooden carving once had stood.

I tried to hide my excitement and, opening my knapsack, gave the little girl and three other children who had suddenly appeared the entire store of my candies. I had won the family's confidence, but the woman could tell me nothing about the doll beyond that her husband had found it in his fields and given it to his youngest daughter for a toy.

I waited for the master of the house to return from the fields. Ali was young, friendly, and without suspicion. He told me how, while plowing five weeks ago, he had come across two wooden dolls. One he had given to his daughter, the other he had presented to the *muktar* of Khan Junis. He knew nothing of the *muktar's* having sold it for a good price in Jerusalem, and hadn't even mentioned the second doll to him. It rather amused him that so prominent a man as the *muktar* should have acted in so greedy and small a manner.

Fragment of Egyptian doll, 2½″ long.

Quickly Ali and I made a deal. Tonight I would be his guest, and tomorrow morning we would go to his field where he would show me the exact spot where he had found the two figurines. I shared their dinner of tomatoes and bread, rolled into the blanket Ali's wife gave me, and was asleep before the first stars came out.

Before sunup we were on our way to the fields. Ali pointed out the furrow, sprouting now with maize, where the two dolls had been uncovered. His topsoil was shallow; whatever was buried beneath it could not be buried very deep. I encircled the spot with stones as markers and assuring the young farmer I would recompense him for any damage done to his crop, we began to dig.

We had penetrated hardly a foot when my shovel struck something hard. I cleared the dirt from a limestone slab one foot high and three quarters of a foot wide which, exquisitely sculptured, showed two Egyptian priests standing under a boat of the dead. The slab had nearly twenty hieroglyphic signs, and I was able to identify it as of the time of the Hebrew patriarchs, with a corresponding Egyptian date of 1600 B.C. The stone was a considerable discovery, for decipherment of the hieroglyphs would tell the story of the tomb it came from.

I continued my digging cautiously, careful not to destroy possible wood objects with the sharp edge of my shovel. But the two-foot level was barren, and I was forced to conclude that the tomb to which the slab belonged had been ransacked some thousands of years ago, and that what I had found was not the exact site of the tomb chamber, but the dumping ground where grave robbers had deposited objects from the tomb they thought worthless.

Such a conclusion is heartbreaking to the archaeologist, but he will often dig on, hoping against hope until dark. We had dug another foot when I saw something glittering in Ali's shovel. It was a gilded sun disk on a wooden stem, two inches in diameter and of the same period as the two wooden figurines. The finding of the disk spurred my energy, and though my hands were covered with blisters I felt no pain or discomfort.

When Ali's wife came with food and a clay jar filled with cool water, the pit was almost three feet deep. We lunched and rested and began to dig again.

Within the next hour I had found a wooden figurine representing a servant, a five-inch wooden model of a sarcophagus with remnants of hieroglyphic writing, and a wooden solar boat one foot long. We dug for another two hours, but without result. The earth had become increasingly harder, and I knew from experience that in such soil, never touched by human hands, there is nothing to be found. I told Ali he could stop digging.

My findings more than pleased me. Here in a maize field between Gaza and Khan Junis I had unearthed remains of the only Egyptian solar boat to be found in Palestine, and other remnants of Egyptian presence going back thirty-five hundred years. Back in Ali's house I sorted and examined my finds more carefully and paid Ali for his help. Finally I convinced his little daughter she should exchange her doll for what delicacies were in my knapsack. It was now late afternoon; I could make my way back to Gaza by donkey, and there find connections to the train to Jerusalem.

Late that night I arrived back in Jerusalem from one of my shortest but most successful excursions. Before dropping in on Ben-Dor at the Museum next morning, I stopped off in the bazaar and bought a beautiful mechanical doll imported from America. The doll could open and close her eyes and shed real tears. I sent it off to Ali's daughter in Khan Junis.

Ben-Dor was out of his office, but I left an invitation for dinner at my house that evening. Father Fleurant and Ben-Goral arrived early, and I told them the story of the solar boat, now neatly mounted on my desk with the figurines and sun disk. When Ben-Dor came I was hidden with my friends behind a door, and we watched him stop in amazement. He cleaned his glasses and looked again.

I came from behind the door, saying, "From Khan Junis. A solar boat

Solar boat, 17½″ long.

from the time of the patriarch Jacob buried in the ground of Canaan. Slightly more definite proof of ancient Egypt's presence and influence in Canaan than the Museum has been able to establish."

Ben-Dor looked at me, his mouth agape. "But how did you find it?" he stammered.

"Ah," I said, "but that is *my* secret."

» VI «

Salome in Stone

ATTEMPTING to verify the New Testament is a difficult and frequently unrewarding task. Unlike the more ancient periods of the Old Testament, Christ's time was one in which many different civilizations and cultures were strongly intermingled and it is not easy to separate them. While Jerusalem is filled with many Christian shrines, it is difficult to specify many of them as authentic, though their geographic locations as noted in the Gospels are correct. Ge-Hinnom, the pool of Siloam, and the temple area high above the Kidron Valley are all sites that existed in the time of Christ. This is true also of the little mosque built on the foundations of the Roman fort, Antonia.

I have included in this chapter two of my experiences with New Testament archaeology, both of which produced objects of considerable historical value.

The archaeological foundations of Christianity as well as the miracles described in the New Testament were constant subjects of discussion when Father Fleurant, Rabbi Ben-Goral, and I got together for one of our regular battles royal. Ben-Goral who, of course, refused to admit Christ's divinity, was generally aggressive about his ideas. Fleurant's chief weapon was his rather infuriating calm; he believed it was his self-control that gave him the advantage. Most often our discussions ended with a heated argument, dawn breaking with no one the victor, and only the line of empty wine bottles to mark the passage of time.

On this particular evening, when Fleurant praised the wine, Ben-Goral was silent. Fleurant remarked, "Even the wine at the marriage at Cana could not have been better."

"Absurd," snapped Ben-Goral.

Father Fleurant turned to him politely. "Did you say something?"

"Your statement is patently absurd," said Ben-Goral loudly.

The battle was on. Fleurant was patronizingly gentle. "What is absurd, my good friend?"

"As if you didn't know!" the rabbi shouted. "I mean all that nonsense about the miracle of Cana."

Fleurant replied with infinite patience. "To me it is a perfectly acceptable miracle."

Ben-Goral shook his head. "There are no miracles."

The old monk turned to me, the palms of his hands uplifted in supplication. "Paul, what shall we do with this poor benighted rabbi? He is stubborn as a mule."

"The marriage at Cana proves no miracle," said Ben-Goral. "It is the sheerest fiction. Either that, or Jesus was only a magician, if a good one."

"A *divine* magician," Fleurant put in quickly. "I see that you concede that much. You are beginning to see the light."

"I have always seen the light," Ben-Goral assured him crossly. "It is you, old man, who are deluded." He laughed contemptuously. "Changing water into wine — that's a fairy tale for children."

"Then it should be within your ken," said Fleurant with irony.

Ben-Goral was furious now. "Listen!" he shouted, pounding on the table, "You and your church maintain that many of your priestly powers were inherited from Jesus through apostolic succession, do you not?"

The monk nodded.

"Then you, Father Fleurant, of the Franciscan order, should be able to duplicate the miracle. Here," he said, pushing a carafe of water in front of Fleurant, "are the means. Let me see you do it."

It seemed to me that Ben-Goral was going a little far, but he pushed away my interceding hand. "Once and for all," he said, "we will settle the question."

My friends needed calming down. I refilled our glasses and said, "Here, we have wine already. Let's drink it." But I was unsuccessful in easing the tension.

"Very well," said Fleurant. He lowered his head as if in prayer. Lifting his hands over the water, he gazed up into the starlit sky. Minutes passed in silence. Then, pouring the contents of the carafe into a glass, he drank it.

"It is wine," he said. "Real wine."

Glowering, Ben-Goral took up the glass and sipped from it. He set the glass down hard. "It is water," he shouted, getting very red, "plain, ordinary water!"

Fleurant cocked his head and drank again. "It is most assuredly wine," he announced to the rabbi. "Even the pleasure a miracle brings is denied you. You are too realistic and earthy, my friend." He pushed the glass towards me. "Paul, you decide." I caught his surreptitious wink.

I sipped from the glass and said, "Yes, it is wine."

Ben-Goral sprang to his feet. "You are both idiots!" Grabbing the glass from my hand he swallowed what was left in noisy gulps and slammed it down on the table. "It is water, and you are fools," he said, and stalked away into the garden.

Father Fleurant rocked with silent laughter.

"Ben-Goral," said Fleurant, when he was himself again, "would make an excellent Christian."

I laughed. "And just the other day he told me you would make a fine Jew."

I refilled our glasses with the wine of Latrum, and we sat waiting for Ben-Goral to return. In a moment he came up from the garden and took his customary chair.

Fleurant smiled. "My friend, I wanted only to prove to you that when we believe, we believe even in miracles. It was water, of course, but thinking of Him, I tasted the sweetness of wine."

"That's better," said Ben-Goral, completely mollified. "But please, don't give me such a shock again. For a moment I took you for one of the holy men."

"I am pleased that you accepted my lesson. If you thought, however fleetingly, I was capable of miracles, then one day you will accept the miracle that is genuine."

They shook hands and were friends again, and we began to talk of the marriage at Cana, related in the second chapter of the Gospel according to St. John. At the wedding, to which Jesus, Mary, and the disciples were invited, the scant supply of wine ran out. Mary asked Jesus to replenish it, and Jesus ordered that six jars be filled with water. The contents of the jars poured out by the servants was wine, and this was Jesus' first known miracle.

Father Fleurant offered the opinion that Mary knew of Jesus' miraculous abilities; otherwise she would not have asked for so public a demonstration of them. It occurred to me that the wedding party in itself must have had some importance, since Jesus had attended it. Among Christians the story of the marriage at Cana has been accepted as fact, but there was no record of it other than the Gospels. I wondered if other evidence was discoverable.

After Fleurant and Ben-Goral had departed arm in arm this possibility continued to intrigue me. I was particularly anxious to find an antiquity from the period of the New Testament, and perhaps prove that the marriage at Cana had actually taken place. Fleurant as a good Christian accepted the Biblical interpretation of the marriage feast; but even he had his doubts of its historical fact. Ben-Goral rejected it entirely. I wanted to prove them wrong if I could. That night I decided upon an expedition to Cana, after planning some thorough historical research.

Ancient Cana existed no longer, but deep in the Galilean foothills was the village of Kufr el-Cana, some ten miles northeast of Nazareth. In the Old Testament Kufr el-Cana is referred to as Gath-hepher, where Jonah the prophet was born. Curiously, archaeologists had paid little attention to the town, though in the closing years of the nineteenth century a German expedition had worked nearby. The little village where Crusaders once had dwelt had long been recognized as one of Christianity's holy shrines, and was now included in the itinerary of all the major pilgrimages.

Some 1,500 people lived there now, two thirds of them Christians, the rest Moslems. Kufr el-Cana had a Moslem mosque, a Greek Orthodox church, and a small Roman Catholic church. Between the two Christian sects a unique rivalry existed. The Roman Catholics claimed their church was built atop an ancient chapel erected by Constantine the Great in the fourth century, in turn built upon the site of the house where the wedding had taken place. On the altar of this church was a plaque with a Latin inscription reading: "Here is the place where the pitchers were."

The Greek Orthodox had on display a wine cup found during excavations for the foundation of their church, and claimed this cup had been used at the wedding and been touched by Christ himself. I knew from my research that both churches could not have been built upon the wedding site. The cup of the Greek Orthodox postdated both in material and ornamentation the time of Christ.

My own starting point was the well of the village market place. In one of his writings, Epiphanius, Bishop of the Eastern church, in Cyprus, who lived around A.D. 375, had mentioned a well close to the house where the couple had been married. According to Epiphanius, every year on the 11th of *Tybi* (April) in the Egyptian calendar the water of Cana turned to wine. For many years, Epiphanius had said, this date was a holiday in the village of Cana.

In a chronicle of the Crusades I had found another reference to Cana. On a certain day of the year a marriage feast was celebrated around the fountain with free wine distributed to the village. This celebration had been banned by the Christian king Isaac I of Jerusalem in the thirteenth century A.D. Isaac, a pious man, had disapproved of the villagers' drunkenness on the day of reverence.

These were the last direct links between Kufr el-Cana and the Gospel of St. John I had been able to find; after A.D. 1250 Cana was no longer mentioned. But I hoped to come across unrecorded folklore among the villagers themselves.

I left Jerusalem, headed north, and arrived in Kufr el-Cana shortly after noon. I found lodgings with a Christian widow and unpacked my knapsack. With books, maps, and papers littered about, my new room looked much like my study in Jerusalem before one of Sonja's determined cleanings. When the place grew gray with cigarette smoke I began to feel completely at home.

That evening I wandered through Kufr el-Cana's crooked streets, speaking to all the graybeards I met, asking them what stories they had heard of the miracle for which their town was famous. The results were meager, and I visited the priests of the two rival Christian churches. They, too, could tell me nothing I did not already know. I realized my task was a hard one. I had my archaeological license from the Department of Antiquities of the British government in Jerusalem, but any digging I might do would be an insult to the priests and the town elders.

The situation called for diplomacy. I bought bagsful of candy at the local confectioner's and distributed them to the children. Through the children I was able to gain the confidence of their parents, and was accepted by them as a more or less scholarly tourist. At the coffeehouse in the market place I played host to the priests, providing food and wine. I was careful not to bring together the Roman Catholics and the Greek Orthodox, for they feared and hated one another like cat and dog.

The foundations of the town had changed little since the time of the Crusades. Taking this into account, I examined the foundation stones of the houses on the market place, and made my first significant discovery. The foundations of several of them were large slabs typical of the

Roman era in the Palestine of two thousand years ago. If the marriage had taken place at all, it had probably been in one of these houses in close proximity to the well.

The evening of the fifth day I had a visitor. He was a middle-aged Arab, friendly but avaricious. I knew he had information to sell, and I pretended disinterest. After the first amenities I fell silent, waiting for him to open the immemorial process of barter.

He spoke finally, saying, "Sir, I know several places where it would profit you to dig." This surprised me; I had told no one in Kufr el-Cana I planned to excavate, making it known only that I had come here in search of material for a book I was writing.

Feigning innocence, I asked him, "Dig for what?"

He smiled broadly. "I know what you look for — gold from the tombs of ancient kings or queens. I can help you. I know where you can find fortunes."

Before I could set the man straight the door opened to reveal a dozen villagers standing in the hallway. Each held something in his hand — a pottery jar, a broken teapot, a kitchen utensil. One hopefully proffered a broken Coca-Cola bottle. They had heard I was looking for relics of the past. I got rid of them finally, distributing small coins right and left. My first visitor required baksheesh of slightly larger denomination.

Now that my purpose in Kufr el-Cana was known, I resolved to take the bull by the horns and approach the owners of the houses in the town built on Roman foundations. I went to see the householder who lived nearest the well. He was a Christian Arab whose name was Hyatt, a textile salesman and local agent for the Singer sewing machine. Hyatt, a man of the Oriental world, was shrewd, successful, and respected as a businessman. I knew he would drive a hard bargain.

He listened to me politely. "Then you wish to dig up my courtyard?" he inquired.

"Only a few feet, preliminarily. If I find indications of what I'm looking for, I would compensate for further excavation."

"My property would be ruined."

"I would pay you well, Mr. Hyatt. And if I am successful, your house will become a shrine and yourself a famous man."

Seemingly disinterested in the delights of fame, Hyatt demanded an exorbitant price for the right to dig near his courtyard wall. Finally we came to an agreement. I paid him three Palestinian pounds — about twelve dollars at the time — with the promise of another nine if I dug further than the minimum two feet. For each additional foot of excavation beyond three feet, Hyatt would receive another two pounds. It occurred to me that should I be successful, Kufr el-Cana might well prove an expensive proposition.

I began work the following day with two of Hyatt's sons and their two cousins as my manual helpers; Hyatt distrusted strangers. Before excavating, I examined the courtyard thoroughly. Along the base of the walls were several clearly ancient Roman stones. There was a definite hump in the soil that extended from the wall into the courtyard. Several things could have caused it, among them an accumulation of rubbish or a natural disturbance. With my pick I broke the soil of the hump, deepening my blows gradually. One foot down, I noticed a change in the soil composition. This was a good sign, meaning that the ground was not uniform and I could expect to find succeeding levels.

I put Hyatt's sons to work digging; the other boys removed the soil in baskets and piled it at one end of the courtyard. There I set up a table and chair where I sieved through the sand, using my magnifying glass at regular intervals.

Within a few hours the ditch from the hump to the courtyard wall was two feet deep, and I had sifted out several pottery shards, some of them three to four hundred years old. Absorbed in my work, I had not noticed the gathering crowd, among it priests from both Catholic and Greek Orthodox churches, standing well apart.

Determined to expand and deepen the excavation ditch, I paid the grumbling Hyatt his additional nine pounds. Three days passed, the work going more slowly as we passed the strata of natural soil and encountered another, grayish and gritty in character. The pottery shards became thicker and cruder, and I came upon fragments of jars and dishes more than a thousand years old.

When in another foot of digging the character of the soil had not changed, I grew impatient. I was afraid the two-thousand-year level could not be reached with less than another five to six feet of excavation. I had already dug five feet and found nothing of importance.

Hyatt's grumbling, unaffected by his increasing profits, grew louder. Again and again I assured him I would restore the excavation and hold myself strictly accountable for any damage to his house and courtyard. My funds were seriously low. Had I listened to reason, I would have packed up then and there. But though the evidence was all against it, my hunch was too compelling. The passion of the gambler drove me and I could not quit now. In the evenings I bolted my frugal meal and went to my room to read and study.

On the seventh day one of the boys shouted in excitement and held up a small clay oil lamp in perfect condition. I ordered the boys to stop digging, in case their shovels broke or destroyed other objects, and hurriedly cleaned the lamp. Clearly marked with gnostic geometrical designs and in construction very primitive, the lamp was typical of the second, third, and fourth centuries in the Holy Land, when Palestine was in religious and political upheaval. Out of this confusion had developed the gnostic philosophy, which can be regarded as the labor pains of organized Christianity. Although in itself not an important find, the lamp was a great reward and encouragement.

From then on I worked with the boys in the excavation ditch. Now almost five and a half feet deep, I was obliged to shore it up carefully. Shovelful by shovelful we dug deeper. I felt sure I was now in a stratum equivalent to the third century A.D.

Then came the second discovery. In one shovelful of dirt I found three beautiful irridescent glass beads, part of a necklace typical of Christ's time. The following morning, at seven feet, we came across three plaster slabs, either street or courtyard pavements. A short time later, on the eastern side of the ditch, I found cubes of Roman limestone mosaic, the original mortar adhering to it. I knew I stood now in the courtyard of a house at least two thousand years old.

A new problem faced me. We were seven feet underground and several feet to the east of where I could expect a continuation of the mosaic floor or wall. We would have to dig a tunnel to it. Every shovelful brought up more mosaic; soon I had over two hundred pieces. When darkness fell we were forced to stop work, but not before our picks had struck blank wall directly beneath the garden wall of Hyatt's courtyard.

I cautioned my excited co-workers. "Please," I said, "don't speak of this. Tell no one."

I bedded down for the night at the excavation, sending one of the boys back to my rooming house for blankets. When I awaked at dawn, I was touched to see that the four boys had crept back to the ditch to sleep near me.

We were eager to resume the excavation. I was haunted by the hope that I had found a house from the time of Christ, perhaps the very dwelling in which the marriage had taken place.

I knew I lacked the proper tools for a thorough excavation. Though I had been careful to shore the tunnel up at regular intervals, it might collapse at any moment, burying alive those of us who were in it at the time. For the right kind of job I needed not only Hyatt's approval of a large-scale excavation but the help of the Palestine Department of Antiquities, the Rockefeller Museum, or one of the universities with which I was loosely connected. It would have been sensible for me to close the site, return to Jerusalem, and organize a more fully staffed expedition. But my excitement was too great for that. I decided to continue the work in the tunnel myself, using the boys only as helpers in the open area of the excavation.

My plan now was to work along the stone wall both right and left, looking for an opening, while the boys built stronger supports for the tunnel walls behind me. It was damp, and the perspiration poured off me in streams as I lay on my stomach, chipping away with my pick at the sand that adhered like cement to the wall. I do not know how long I lay there, clawing away, seven feet underground without safe buttressing. But suddenly my pick encountered no resistance. I had hit upon a sand-choked opening, either a window or doorway.

I returned to the tunnel opening for a small shovel and a basket, and at the wall once more, began to shovel the loose sand away from the opening. After another four hours of work, I was able to determine that the opening was the entrance to a room. By late afternoon I had succeeded in clearing an opening that measured two by three feet. I could now effect a passage into the room, though the rain of loose dirt from overhead discouraged me from going further. I stopped for the day.

The next morning, after another two hours of shoveling, I broke into the room. It was a small chamber, probably a storeroom, three yards by two and with a ceiling five feet from the floor. There were no windows. The room seemed completely empty, until my flashlight revealed a clay ossuary, about two feet long and one and a half feet wide. Such chests were used from 300 B.C. to A.D. 300 to hold the bones of the more illustrious dead and their valuable belongings. The chest was decorated with circular symbols typical of the first century.

The lid was sealed to the chest with mortar; I would be able to open it only above ground with the proper tools. After shoving the chest into the mouth of the tunnel, I took one last look around the room. Then I made my way back through the tunnel to the ditch, pushing the ossuary inch by inch before me. The boys lifted it by rope from the ditch to Hyatt's courtyard.

I took up a chisel, and chipped away at the sealing mortar, warning the excited boys that what the chest contained might not be a pleasant sight. My own heart was pounding as I pried off the lid.

There were no bones in the chest, but under a thick layer of dust two glass cups and a large glass dish in perfect condition. Seldom had I seen such perfection in glass-making. Perspiring more profusely now than I had while working in the tunnel, I asked myself: Could these

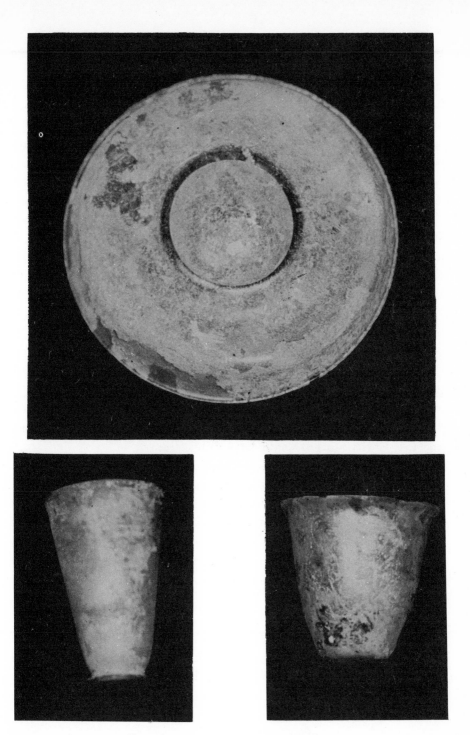

Two glass cups and large glass plate.

cups have been used at the marriage feast Christ attended? Certainly their original owner had thought them extraordinary enough to warrant preservation.

Two days later I was back in Jerusalem, and that evening Fleurant, Ben-Goral, Sukenik, and my other colleagues came to see my find. Never before, they said, had there been such a discovery in Cana. I had proved again that lone-wolf archaeology brought results.

Later the two men of God and I sat on my porch drinking the red Judean wine Ben-Goral had presented to me with his congratulation. I told them of the excavation, and then I posed aloud the question that haunted us all: had the cups indeed been used at the marriage feast?

"It is obvious," said Father Fleurant, "that this glassware was used at the marriage. Otherwise, their owner would have had no reason to preserve it so carefully."

Ben-Goral only smiled.

"Undoubtedly," continued the Father, "there were other cups and plates, but they were given away to the guests as mementos."

Fleurant picked up one of the cups and regarded it with adoring eyes. "To think," he said softly, "that this glass held the miraculous wine, and that Christ himself could have drunk from it."

Though the good Father may have been convinced, as a scientist I was required to be more skeptical. The Cups of Cana were of the time of Christ and from the town He had visited; perhaps one had touched His lips. But of this I could not be dogmatically certain, nor could anyone. It was miracle enough for me that I should have been able to kindle so bright a light as that which shone now in the eyes of my holy friend.

2

One hot afternoon, in a shade-drawn hotel room near the Sea of Galilee, something white gleamed in the hand of a bronzed and wrinkled Arab sitting across the room from me. In the semidarkness the object took on a definite form, and I felt an almost unendurable excitement.

To hide it I motioned to the Arab to set the piece aside, and return to the coins and glass beads he had already shown me. My cigarette trembled in my hand as I discussed the beads in Arabic with my visitor. Now and then I stole a look at the white object lying on a piece of crumpled newspaper on the tile floor. I could hardly refrain from snatching it up and hurrying away with it. For two years I had waited for this moment, and these last few minutes were agony.

At last we struck a bargain. The Arab left full of joviality and fervent wishes for more such profitable business meetings. I closed the door quickly, bolted it, and picked up the piece. It was a small head of marble no bigger than a woman's fist. The patina of time had tinted it with a soft, ivory-like luster. It was plainly the portrait of a young woman; of a princess, judging by the tiara or diadem she wore. I knew where the head had been found, I knew the period from which it dated, and as I turned it over in my hands, feeling its smoothness and admiring its enigmatic perfection, I dared to ask myself the question: was I holding the likeness of a Herodian princess of Judea, perhaps even Salome, who had danced before Herod and his court and received into her hand the severed head of John the Baptist?

To understand the intensity of my emotion it is necessary to go back some two years. At that time, on a visit to the Dominican Church of Domitio on the Mount of Zion, I saw an interesting new addition to the church's archaeological collection of artifacts from Northern Palestine. This was a large pottery wine jar of Roman times found, so Father Andreas the custodian had told me, near the ruins of Herod Antipas' palace in Machaerus, far south of Tiberias toward the Dead Sea. The jar had been found by an Arab farmer, in a cave near where he had been plowing, as often happens in the Holy Land. The jar's period could be definitely assigned by a number of coins found in it dating from A.D. 4 to 49.

Constantly on the lookout as I was for such finds, I asked to see the coins. Father Andreas showed me one, in bad condition, known to have been struck by Herod. The Arab had found other objects in the jar but had refused to sell them, although describing them to the priest as "trash."

The word "trash" can mean a great deal to the archaeologist, and the pottery jar aroused my curiosity. I sensed immediately that the things the Arab had wanted to keep were of greater value than the jar itself. Father Andreas did not know the name or village of the farmer, something for which I had no right to blame him. He was a theologian, not an archaeologist, and his little museum was not designed for scholarship and research.

A pottery jar from the time of Herod; the report of an Arab who had found it, name and habitation unknown; certain other objects found in the jar, nature and number unknown. I had run down more than one archaeological find with less information to go on, and I set to work.

My first step was to find out the name and village of the farmer. As an aid I could count on my twenty-year acquaintance among the Arab farmers in the valleys, the shepherds in the mountains, the desert Bedouins. The time was World War II, and I was with the British Information Office, my job to help spread the Allied cause among the Arabs and prevent an Arab-Nazi alliance. My duties took me over the length and breadth of Palestine, and in the course of my travels I threw out a network of inquiry regarding the unknown Arab *fellah.*

Many names were brought to me by my Arab friends in the next six or seven months. I investigated every likely prospect, going miles out of my way to the western shore of Lake Tiberias and along the River Jordan. But the trail became fainter. Finally, eight months after I had first seen the pottery jar in the museum of Domitio, I found my man. He was a relatively well-to-do Arab who owned farm land in El-Hammi, in the vicinity of Tiberias, and near the village of Pelah on the Transjordan side of the River Arnon. He spent most of his time in El-Hammi.

Finding him was only the start of a long and tedious process inevitable in dealing with the primitive people of the Middle East. Mussa was stockily dignified in appearance, with a face heavily pock-marked and bronzed from the Galilean and Moabit suns. His age was indefinite; time means little to such dwellers in the wilderness.

Mussa was in no haste to deal with me. Ten times I visited his village, to discuss everything from the weather to the state of the camel market and the high price of figs before he would tell me what beside the coins he had found in the jar near the ancient Herodian palace-fortress of Machaerus. Finally, he said, "There were some beads, and other trash." I pressed for a chance to see the trash and finally he agreed to bring it to me at Tiberias on my next trip north.

As soon as my official duties permitted I made plans to return to Tiberias, and sent word to Mussa in El-Hammi that I would be at the Tiberias Hotel on a certain day. On that day I arrived, and for three days I waited, busy meanwhile in the neighboring Galilean villages on behalf of the Allied Information Office in Jerusalem.

When I had begun to give up hope Mussa arrived. We went immediately to my room. The blinds were drawn against the sun and the room was shadowy. I ordered coffee and shared a cup with my guest. I was smoking cigarettes, but Mussa declined one. I ordered a *narghile* for him and we sat talking of irrelevant things, drinking coffee at intervals as the day wore on.

When I tactfully brought the subject around to the purpose of Mussa's visit he said, "Yes, *Chawadjah*, I have brought some things with me," and promptly digressed again. He was going to keep me dangling.

On the floor beside him stood a wicker basket in which were, I was sure, the pieces he had brought me. Finally, with a sigh, he opened the basket and rummaged around in it. I caught a glimpse of his lunch — Arab bread, tomatoes, and onions — a pair of sandals he had brought to town to be mended for one of his wives, and a rolled-up Arabic newspaper.

With an air of dignified unconcern he first handed me several ancient bronze coins like the one Father Andreas had shown me. They were from the Herodian period. Only one coin was interesting, though not valuable; many like it had been found in the last fifty years. I passed along the information to Mussa in a casual tone, to discourage him from asking an exorbitant price for the other articles.

"I assume these were found in the Roman jar you sold to the Domitio?" I asked.

"Yes," replied Mussa, "and also other things." He took a twist of newspaper from the wicker basket, and unrolling it, poured out a handful of finely irridescent glass beads.

The bubbling water of his *narghile* sounded softly in the room as I examined the beads. Some were blue, some yellow, some green, some opalescent; originally clear, they were covered now by a blue and silver patina. I placed them as of approximately the same period as the coins; they had their value, but were hardly worth a two-year search.

Then, for the third time, Mussa reached into his basket and drew out a small object wrapped in crumpled newspaper. Quickly he unrolled it, and a white object gleamed. "Something hardly worth showing," he said, "just a piece of infidel filth." The only reason he had brought it along was because one of his wives had demanded he get rid of the unclean thing, lest it contaminate the house.

Among the fanatically religious Moslems any representation of the human face or figure in painting or sculpture is considered blasphemous, and any representation of the female face or figure is held to be obscene. The very orthodox Jews observe the same taboo today. In the time of Moses it was forbidden to make a likeness of a human being since human beings are made in the likeness of God.

My excitement, as Mussa showed me the sculpted head, I have already described. It seemed an eternity till Mussa left and I was free to examine my prize at the window. The first signs certainly pointed toward its being a Herodian princess. The words of the Gospel flashed through my mind: "The daughter of Herodias danced before the company, and pleased Herod, so that he promised with an oath to give her whatever she might ask. Prompted by her mother, she said, Give me the head of John the Baptist here on a platter. And the king was sorry; but because

"Head of Salome," 4$\frac{1}{10}$" *high.*

of his oaths and his guests he commanded it to be given her; he sent and had John beheaded in the prison, and his head was brought on a platter and given to the girl, and she brought it to her mother" (Matt. 14:6-11, *RSV*).

Salome! Could this possibly be an actual portrait of the girl celebrated in art and legend for almost two thousand years? About whom scores of great painters had created their own imagined likenesses: Titian, Rubens, Cranach, Ghirlandajo, da Volterra, Moreau, Vasari, Henner, Leuni, Veneto? This woman's legend had inspired Oscar Wilde's masterpiece, set to music by Richard Strauss, translated into a dozen languages and sung in every capital of the civilized world. In her celebration, poems, dramas, and novels had appeared in every country of the Occident.

I studied the head, with its sightless eyes and muted lips, and I became convinced that it was indeed the portrait in stone of, if not Salome herself, at the least a Herodian princess.

Historic fact tended to bear me out. Herod had resided in Tiberias, but lived most of the time in his palace-stronghold of Machaerus. Though in the Gospels the place of John the Baptist's imprisonment for sedition is not specifically named, in legendary accounts the place of his incarceration and death is assumed to be Machaerus, where Herod celebrated his birthday with a great feast at which Salome danced. The execution was pictured as taking place immediately afterward, as in the Bible, and many imaginative recreations of the scene had Salome continuing her dance holding the severed head aloft in her hands. A more precise authority, Flavius Josephus, in his *Antiquities of the Jews,* has Machaerus situated not near Tiberias — up to the last fifty years generally considered by scholars to be its location — but farther south on the Dead Sea, "on the borders of the dominions of Aretas, King of Arabia; Petrea; and the dominions of Antipas." It was here and not near Tiberias that Mussa had found the pottery jars.

I telephoned immediately to Jerusalem to Ben-Dor and Olaf Madson, the latter a leading authority on Biblical antiquities. Their excitement was equal to mine. "Stay where you are," they told me, "we'll drive to Tiberias by special car tomorrow." I spent the next day in a nervous dream, counting the minutes to their arrival. They came at dinner time and, postponing the evening meal, we rechecked the statue's identification. Early the next morning we went to El-Hammi to interrogate Mussa. At first the old man thought I had returned for my money, but once assured of my good faith he repeated the story of how he had found the jar, describing the exact location of the site, and swearing to Allah that he had given me everything that was in the jar. He declared himself perfectly willing to show us the cave where he had discovered the jar.

It was a three-hour trip by car to the Arab village now called Mekaur, situated some four hundred yards from Machaerus' circumvailing wall. The ruins of Machaerus sit upon the top of a conical hill rising about twenty-eight hundred feet above the Dead Sea in the hills of Moab. Inside the crumbled walls we found a dried-out well and two dungeons. One of these may well have been the prison in which John was confined on the charge of inciting to rebellion.

It was too late for further exploration, and we stayed the night in Mussa's clay house. We bought vegetables, rice, and eggs from the villagers, and Ben-Dor, an excellent cook, prepared an attractive meal. Soon after daybreak, Mussa brought us to the cave where he had found the wine jar, about eighty feet from the remains of the northern fortress wall. Madson discovered three or four Roman quader stones once used as pavement for a path leading directly from the fortress to the cave. Later we found more quader stones, serving as house foundations for the Arabs of the village.

We had no doubt that Mussa had found the pottery jar in the cave, probably used by the people of the fortress as a hiding place. But who, we wondered, had hidden it there nearly eighteen centuries ago? Had the jar and its contents been stolen from the fortress and buried by the thief? Antiquarians can only theorize on this point; who can say?

Back in Tiberias we re-examined the statue. Its origin was established definitely enough. Machaerus had been occupied mainly during the reign of Herod. Shortly after the brutal murder of John, King Aretas had routed Herod's armies and destroyed it. Machaerus was never rebuilt. The statue's thrice indented royal diadem also had its significance: the typical sign of royalty, it denoted the imperial rank of its wearer. The most important aspect of the diadem was the knot at its back; only royalty had the right to fasten its diadems in this manner. Herod was an Edomite and, becoming King of the Jews, was bound to adhere to Hebrew rites and traditions. The most important of these was that a Hebrew must not have made a likeness of himself. Thousands of Hebrews had been killed in the Temple of Jerusalem when they refused to bow down before a sculpture of the Roman Emperor. No coin was ever struck or circulated in Judea or Galilee bearing the Emperor's portrait. Though portrait sculpture was in vogue among the high officials of the Roman Empire, it was forbidden in the land of the Jews. Salome, who did not follow Judean religious laws, who had been partly educated in Rome and influenced by Roman culture and civilization, had possibly had her portrait clandestinely chiseled either in Tiberias or Machaerus.

We agreed that the statue could not have been the work of Greek or Roman artisans. Its modeling was too primitive; it was neither a typical likeness of Venus or Aphrodite nor were its features those of a Greek or a Roman goddess. The head was the work of a local artist in Salome's time, we were certain; its marble was identical with many marble columns found in various parts of Palestine in the Herodian period. Because of its small size, it could be hidden easily when Hebrew dignitaries or noblemen visited Herod's court. Perhaps the owner of the sculpture had used the wine jar as a hiding place for her forbidden likeness. It was possible that both statue and necklace had been taken from the palace in Machaerus by a young man attached to the retinue of Salome and hidden in the cave nearby as a memento of his beloved, the coins included as a votive offering to please the gods.

Who can say?

On strictly scientific grounds it is obvious that no irrefutable identification of the statue as a likeness of Salome can be made. The archaeological enigma has been summed up by a number of scholars as follows:

"The head is certainly a portrait of a royal person. It is therefore likely that it is the portrait of a Herodian Princess." — Dr. R. Ben-Dor, Curator, Rockefeller Museum, Jerusalem.

"I fully believe this to be the head of a woman of high rank of Herodian times. The head was found in Machaerus and was executed by a local sculptor of the time. All indications point to it as a portrait of Salome." — G. Olaf Madson, Curator of Palestinian Antiquities, Royal Museum, Stockholm.

"The head is easily recognizable as that of a princess of Herodian times. The one such princess named in history and described in the Bible is Salome. The age of the subject of this portrait precludes its identification with Herodias (Herod's wife), or any such matronly Queen. The period is identical with that of Salome and Herod Antipas." — Professor Eugene Stolzer, noted collector of Palestinian antiquities, architect, builder of the Habima Theater in Tel-Aviv.

"From all appearances and from composition studies it is the head of a princess of the period of Herod. It has an air of majesty." — Dr. Samuel M. Segal, Biblical scholar, Rabbi of Mount Neboh Congregation, New York City.

"In my opinion a portrait. The most convincing features to me are the lower lip which is highly personalized, and the subject's strange smile." — Dr. Stephen Kayser, Director, Jewish Museum, New York.

"The work is neither Greek nor Roman, nor is it archaic. The features show many naturalistic (i.e., portrait) touches. The placement of the ears alone is most unusual and a definite sign of personification." — Dr. Gisela Richter, Curator of Greek and Roman Art, Metropolitan Museum of Art, New York City.

» VII «

The Luck Factor

I HAVE grouped five of my finds together in this chapter not because they are linked culturally — they come from widely diverse periods of history — but because of the bizarre ways in which I located them. These five objects — the sandstone snake, the mask, the ivory fragment, the lotus leaf, and the ring of the Empress Julia Domna — are good examples of the part that luck plays in the life of an archaeologist.

As I have hinted previously, a good archaeologist is something of a gambler at heart. Despite months of painstaking research, failure is almost certain without a generous handful of luck. A basic research plan can seem foolproof and then the digging turn into a total flop because the tomb, or temple, or city wall was missed by a few feet. In still more extreme cases, a wrong road, an overheard word, an impulsive gesture of friendship have brought to light priceless treasures that might otherwise have remained buried in the sands of Palestine or in a pile of rubble in the backyard of an Arab farmer.

In the case of a free-lance archaeologist the luck factor is particularly vital. For example, the discovery of the snake and the mask was in no way due to the research I had done for a trip north of Jerusalem where, I believed, the first Sumerian settlers had entered Canaan. Instead, they were the result of an aged Arab woman's instinctive trust in me.

I had been planning this trip for some time. My research had revealed that the Sumerians of Mesopotamia, whose civilization had flourished a thousand years before the Babylonians in the earliest Biblical times, had sent tribesmen to the Judean mountains of Canaan. But little was known of these people, and I had to base the bulk of my investigations upon legend, folklore, and saga.

The name "Canaan" occurs in the Bible for the first time in Genesis: "Terah took Abram his son and Lot the son of Haran, his grandson, and Sarai his daughter-in-law, his son Abram's wife, and they went forth together from Ur of the Chaldeans to go into the land of Canaan; but when they came to Haran, they settled there" (11:31, *RSV*).

Canaan possibly means "the land of purple." F. Turvill-Petre's turn-of-the-century explanation of the name's origin is still generally accepted. The Canaanites manufactured a purple dye from the murex shellfish found along the coast, and bartered it to early Pharaonic Egypt and Babylonian royalty several hundred years before Abraham (around 2600 B.C.). Canaan constituted a buffer between Babylonia, Assyria (Mesopotamia), and Egypt. The history of Palestine has always been intimately associated with that of her more powerful neighbors, and this situation exists even today.

Important anthropological discoveries have been made in Canaan in the Stone and Bronze ages, the last approximately ten thousand years before the period of Abraham. Most significant were those of Turvill-Petre, who in 1925 found the "Galilee skull" in the Robber's Cave near the Galilean Sea. In the 1930's human fossils of Paleolithic times were found in Wadi el-Mughara, at Mount Carmel.

The sandstone snake and the mask come from the vicinity of Gezer, in the Judean mountains, where the famous archaeologist R. A. McAllister explored Stone Age caves in 1905 and thus inaugurated organized archaeology in Palestine. In Gezer and in Jerusalem as well, caves were found that were once the workshops of the first potters of the Holy Land. This primitive pottery graphically depicts the cultural standards of the Stone Age.

The facts I was able to gather about the Sumerians themselves were meager and sometimes no longer credible. Layard, in his *Babylon and Nineveh,* had erroneously noted that in Canaan the Sumerians lived in walled cities and fortresses. History records that around 2300 B.C. they were subdued by Semitic tribes under the leadership of Sargon I. Three hundred years later the Elamites conquered Ur, the current Sumerian capital, and the Sumerians as a nation gradually vanished. However, both written and material evidence of their advanced culture continued to influence succeeding civilizations for several centuries.

I had gathered other odd bits of information. Among the later Sumerians there had been an interesting social change from patriarchy to matriarchy, in which hegemony of the tribe was transferred from the oldest man to the oldest woman. The idea of the Amazon state in Greek mythology may have been based in part on Sumerian civilization. I hoped that the legend and folklore of the local Arabs in a town called Der el-Sheik, the village nearest Gezer, would fill in some of the historic gaps, and provide me with clues pointing to a likely spot for excavation in Gezer. This was, practically speaking, unlikely, since evidence of the past as far back as five thousand years ago is seldom found. But my intuition was strong and I felt that there was a good chance that a visit to this particular town would yield something.

The sandstone snake that I found vindicated my intuition. It is particularly interesting archaeologically because of the serpent's symbolism in the Sumerian (and other) cultures of the period. I shall elaborate on this point later in this chapter. The mask is a rare treasure because it is recognized as the only existing likeness of an actual Sumerian, a man who walked the earth some three thousand years before Christ. It is probably the face of a tribal leader, and its headdress is typically Sumerian.

When I left for Gezer I told no one in Jerusalem of my destination, because I knew my friends would discourage my going into an area where the natives were unusually backward and were hostile to people from the outside world. The caves and ruins of Gezer were in a district seething with friction between Arab, Briton, and Zionist. Arabs of this part of Palestine had managed somehow to hold themselves more aloof from the progress of modern times than other communities, and they resented visitors.

I expected to be in Der el-Sheik for seven days. I took my sleeping bag, small coin for the usual bribes, candy for the children and, optimistically, the tools of my trade. The train brought me to Bittir, an Arab village several miles from Jerusalem. A thousand years ago Bittir had been a fortress of the Crusades, and a thousand years before that the Maccabees had held it successfully against the Roman armies of Vespasian.

In Bittir I bought a donkey and headed into the mountains of Judea. It was twilight when I got to Der el-Sheik, a primitive village whose houses were made of raw rock from the mountains, lending to the place the ancient atmosphere of the Bible. The village was dominated by the high minaret of a mosque. I went there, expecting to find the village elders, but instead I was shown into the presence of a young sheik of about twenty-five.

He had a spare red beard and a bad complexion; behind his thick glasses were the glittering eyes of a religious fanatic. Despite my first doubts, I thought it a stroke of luck to encounter a man whose age was so close to my own. I had learned that to have a sheik as a friend meant acceptance in an Arab village, and I hoped this young man would understand my problems and be willing to help.

When I spoke to him in Arabic he replied in French, scathingly. "I don't wish to speak to an infidel in the holy language of the Koran. Men like you aren't worthy of using the Moslem tongue." He glared at me.

I was shocked. I had never encountered such hatred in an Arab. I knew of the Arabs' deep resentment against foreigners, of their explosive nationalism; but this was a particularly insulting and virulent example.

Replying in French I said, "Your feelings are unjustified. Doesn't every sheik who has studied his Koran know that Allah's first law for human relations is love, not hate?" I quoted to him from the Koran on hospitality, but he continued to stare at me stonily.

It seemed pointless for me to ask him for food and lodging, but the prospect of returning to Bittir was unattractive. "Listen to me," I said sharply. "I want to spend the night in Der el-Sheik. Whether you like it or not, I fully intend to stay in this area until I'm ready to move on."

He blinked in surprise; no one, evidently, had ever spoken to him in this manner. "Furthermore," I went on, "I'm tired and thirsty, and I'd like something to drink."

He bowed stiffly, disappeared into a side room, and returned with a tin cup of water. I sniffed it to let the sheik know I was wary of poison. Then I laughed and drank it down.

"This is ridiculous," I told him. "Here we are, two intelligent men snapping at each other because our religions happen to be different. I am a harmless archaeologist; all I want to do is spend a few days in your village gathering scientific data."

Though he didn't smile, his tone was less hostile as he said, "Only the *muktar* can decide if you can stay and where you might sleep. I will take you to him. But first we must go to my house."

At the sheik's house I noted the absence of a women's quarter. He explained that he was unmarried, and excusing himself, left the room. I was surprised to see the large number of books on his shelves. Most were in Arabic, but there were many volumes in French, among them biographies of Napoleon, Cromwell, Lincoln, and Washington. I was impressed. For all I knew I had met a man of strong nationalistic ambitions who dreamed of becoming the next *Mufti* of Jerusalem.

The house of the *muktar* was near the sheik's. A man in his sixties, the *muktar* had a stern face and an eye badly infected by trachoma. When he had heard my story, he immediately stepped aside with the sheik for a whispered conference. The *muktar* then approached me, asking an endless series of seemingly bland but pointed questions. Why had I come alone? What was my real purpose here? What did I expect to find in the caves at Gezer?

Outside my donkey brayed. "Can you see that my animal is watered?" I asked. "He's been dry for hours."

The men looked at one another uncertainly. "It's all right," I said, "he's an Arab donkey."

They left the room. I stepped to the door, looking for a way to escape, but three giant Arabs blocked my path. I was a prisoner.

It was almost an hour before the sheik and the *muktar* returned. With them was a woman I took to be in her seventies. Six feet tall, she was as broad and strong as a man and wore a single garment of blue hand-woven linen embroidered in red. She stared me down, her proud, piercing eyes making me feel like an intruding insect.

"This," said the *muktar*, "is my mother, Arana."

The woman, evidently the village matriarch, was older than I had thought, but her air of regal authority and the straight-backed confidence with which she carried herself made her seem no older than her son.

Arana began to question me in detail, though it was obvious the *muktar* had already told her the relevant facts. I went through the entire explanation again, adding that I wished to be brought before the British police.

"I am the police of Der el-Sheik," the *muktar* said.

Though Arana had given no sign that she accepted my story, she noticed my fatigue. She said, "You will spend the night here. We will talk again in the morning."

They left me frightened and hungry; the guards had already taken my knapsack with its food supply, and for twelve hours I had not eaten. In a moment the sheik returned with a small basket of food and placed it before me, ignoring my pleas for an explanation of his hostile treatment.

The basket contained a jar of sour milk, two *pittas* (the round flat Arabic bread), onions, and a hard piece of goat cheese. I craved a cup of coffee, but there was none. After wolfing down the food, I was exhausted enough to sleep on the spot, but the guards had also taken the sleeping bag from me. I shouted to one of the giants, who brought me the bag.

"Where's the knapsack?" I asked.

"You can't have it."

The firmness of his refusal left no room for discussion. I stretched the sleeping bag out on the floor, slid into it, and closed my eyes. At dawn I awakened and went to the door, from which I could see the guards squatting against the tree in the courtyard. Before I could think of escape one rose to his feet threateningly and I returned inside.

An hour later Arana appeared, carrying a brass cup filled with coffee, with the *muktar* and the young sheik behind her. The coffee, first hot nourishment I had had in two days, was delicious. Arana waited until I was finished. Then she said, "We distrust you, as we distrust anyone who comes to our village from Jerusalem. We will not sell our land at any price. Even if the whole of Palestine is ruled by infidels, Der el-Sheik will remain Arabic."

As I had suspected, they had taken me for an agent of the Arabs in Jerusalem, who bought land and then resold it to the Zionists. I assured them they were mistaken.

The young sheik said, "We have only your word for the purpose of your visit."

"Let me know the names of those Arabs you know in Jerusalem," the *muktar* said. "We will make inquiries."

Unfortunately, the names of my Arab friends in Jerusalem would have meant nothing to the *muktar*. Turning to the sheik I said in French, "What must I do to convince you I am here on a scientific expedition? I don't want to buy your land. I only want to talk with some elder of your village, and perhaps hire a few of your men to work with me at the ruins of Gezer. Once my work is done I'll leave Der el-Sheik, and never come back."

The sheik looked doubtful, but the *muktar* motioned him and Arana to the next room, from where I could hear the mutter of their voices. The *muktar* came back alone.

"What would you pay the workers if we provided them for you?"

"What would you expect?"

"Sixty *piasters* a day."

Sixty *piasters* was almost three dollars, a ridiculously high sum. Ten *piasters* would have been sufficient, and I said so.

"That is my price," said the *muktar*.

His demand had been made to discourage me. Playing the game his way, I said, "Then sixty it is."

His eyebrows arched in surprise. "Have you the money?"

In typical secretive Arab fashion I turned, and with my back to the *muktar*, I pulled out the money pouch hidden under my shirt. I took out a five-pound note and showed it to him. This convinced the old man, who quickly left to make arrangements. A half hour later my donkey awaited me outside the building, my knapsack on his back. Three men had been assigned to accompany me on foot. As we left the village I saw neither Arana, the young sheik, nor the *muktar*, and despite my success I was wary as we reached the foothills.

It was possible the *muktar* had ordered his men to murder me in the hills and return with my donkey and money pouch. They looked villainous enough in their dirty burnouses, scowls on their faces and daggers at their belts. But somehow I felt Arana would never permit such a plan, and as we continued into the foothills I felt more at ease.

It was an hour's journey to the plateau of Gezer, an area of about a thousand by fifteen hundred feet, most of it heavily covered by scrub. The plateau was surrounded by a wall of hills ranging from fifty to two hundred feet. It was perfect for military defense, and many battles had been fought here in the reign of King David. "And after this there arose war with the Philistines at Gezer; then Sibbecai the Hushathite slew Sippai, who was one of the descendants of the giants; and the Philistines were subdued" (I Chronicles 20:4, *RSV*).

Long before David, Gezer had been a Canaanite town, one of the number mentioned in the Tell el-Amarna tablets of the fifteenth century B.C. The tablets had noted Gezer as not far distant from the city of

Lachish and the lower Beth-horon. But it is in the Bible that we find the earliest mention of Gezer: "Then Horam king of Gezer came up to help Lachish; and Joshua smote him and his people, until he had left none remaining" (Joshua 10:33, *RSV*). "To them were given Shechem, the city of refuge for the slayer, with its pasture lands in the hill country of Ephraim, Gezer with its pasture lands" (Joshua 21:21, *RSV*).

Later Gezer was captured from the Canaanites by one of the Pharaohs, and burned. The ruins were rebuilt as a dowry by the Pharaoh to Solomon, when Solomon married one of the Pharaoh's daughters. The town had importance in the wars of the Maccabees. Bacchides the Maccabean strengthened its fortifications (I Maccabees 9:52), and after being besieged and taken by Simon it was made stronger than before.

Clermont Ganneau had done extensive excavation in the Roman level of Gezer. One of the inscriptions he found was from the time of Herod the Great, and marked the city limits of Gezer in Hebrew letters. My own interest in Gezer went further back; I was looking for remnants of the pre-Canaanite civilization that antedated the Roman period by two thousand years.

I saw to the east the caves that I believed had been the living quarters of the very early tribes. I dismounted from my donkey and first reconnoitered the plain; I discovered in a far corner a number of huge stone dolmens, the first monuments created for religious worship. These tall shafts of rock had probably been built eight to ten thousand years ago, long before recorded history. They were starkly primitive, yet I saw in them a resemblance to the Gothic spire, the Moslem minaret, the Egyptian obelisk. Long before Yahweh had become the center of the world of theology, tribesmen reaching for the unknown had erected these monuments. Who these people were, how they had lived, and what they believed are unsolved mysteries.

Perhaps the dolmens had been built by the people whom the Sumerians had conquered. At the base of the dolmens was a floor of flat, warped stone, probably the foundations of a very ancient temple. Grass, weeds, and thorny plants had forced their way through cracks in the floor. What catastrophe, I wondered, had wiped out the existence of these people from the book of mankind?

The openings of the caves were a few feet above the ground, and I asked one of the Arabs to give me a helping boost. He shook his head.

"You must not enter here. The caves are taboo. Our *muktar* could not have known you meant to investigate them."

As a stranger I was doubly bound to the district's laws of superstition, but having come this far I refused to let them hold me back.

"Your own ancestors probably lived in these caves," I replied. "Perhaps I'll find interesting things to tell you about them."

"You lie!" the Arab shouted. "Only Affrit lives here!"

"I tell you there is no devil," I said. "There are only those human devils who act in his name."

"There is a devil. He is the ruler of the snakes. It's death to enter the caves," the Arab insisted.

I shrugged, and strode away to a nearby hilltop. Further argument seemed pointless. I could only hope to return alone to the caves tomorrow.

From the hilltop I noticed patches of *khirbe*, the gray-brown soil discolored by a substratum of decay — usually bones, clay, and remnants of other organic matter. To the archaeologist such areas, the refuse heaps of past civilizations, can be troves of treasure. I started to dig through the *khirbe*, and had no luck at first; the Arabs became impatient and started to grumble. After several hours, I began to uncover pottery shards that had never known the potter's wheel. Of clay, hand-made and sunbaked, they proved that human beings had lived here long before the time of Ephraim, ancestor of one of the twelve tribes of Israel, in whose era men in this part of the world had perfected their primitive arts of farming, weaving, and wheeled pottery. These shards indicated that somewhere on the plateau of Gezer I might be able to find evidence of a primitive civilization.

I took a last look around the plateau to fix in my mind its principal features for the notes and sketches I would make that night, and we returned to the village.

That night Arana, unaccompanied, brought me my dinner. She inquired about the pottery shards I had collected, and when I showed them to her she shook her head pityingly. How could such refuse have any meaning for me? I told her what I knew of life on the plateau in ancient times, and she listened attentively. Now was my chance to ask her, the matriarch of her tribe, what tales she had to tell.

"How," I asked, "did Affrit come to live in the caves of Gezer?"

In her colorful language Arana spoke of how, thousands of years in the past, a huge snake had lived in the mountains; a snake so long that its tail touched the clouds. Fire and steam issued from its mouth, and for generations it had been the scourge of the countryside, striking without warning, destroying the forests, the farms, the villages. The people tried to appease the monster by worshiping it. They built temples in its name and declared feast days in tribute. But the snake remained implacable until Mohammed came to Gezer, conquered it, and locked the snake forever in the caves. There the devil-god remained a prisoner, but able to devour all who came within its reach.

The symbolism-filled story fascinated me. I asked the old woman to tell me others, but she was anxious to get back to the main house, and left me. I started on my notes and sketches, marking the places I wanted to investigate the next day. I returned my papers to the knapsack and prepared my sleeping bag.

Arana's talk had given me an important clue to a number of ancient symbolic writings, and even to esoteric legends of the Bible itself. It occurred to me that the ability of man to make fire was, archaeologically speaking, comparatively recent. There is no document that tells us when man first discovered fire, but long before he tamed it, fire — caused either by spontaneous combustion or lightning — had existed. Afraid of fire, man was ignorant of the way to fight it. When lightning destroyed his forests and hunting grounds and fields, his cave dwellings became

Sandstone snake, 5½″ long, 2¾″ wide.

useless. He could only move away, in search of other fields and forests.

Lightning, then, was an enemy. Within the scope of primitive man's intelligence, he could grasp lightning's magnitude only by comparing it to something he knew from personal experience. Lightning had familiar characteristics. It struck without warning, unpredictably, and in its zigzag from heaven to earth resembled the movement of a snake. To primitive man lightning *was* a snake. And since there was no defense against it, so the snake became to mankind the symbol of evil, of the mysterious and unknown.

The snake was chosen to symbolize the evil that tempted Adam and Eve to their fall. And when God wished to show his displeasure with the chosen people, He sent a horde of fiery serpents among them. In older legends, not incorporated into the Bible, we learn of the snake as the symbol of evil, and in more recent centuries we have such tales as St. George and the Dragon and St. Patrick's chasing the snakes out of Ireland.

Man has come to understand lightning and no longer fears it. But he has never outgrown his fear of evil. The snake remains the symbol of evil and the animal men fear most, despite the fact that among all wild animals it is the easiest to destroy. Mohammed had caged the Affrit, but the primitive villagers of Der el-Sheik still believed the mighty snake was their enemy.

When Arana brought my coffee the following morning I asked her politely when I could return to the plateau. A look of doubt passed across her face and she was about to speak when the young sheik burst into the room. He slapped me across the mouth and launched into a torrent of vituperative Arabic.

"You lied to us!" he cried. "We've seen your drawings and your sketches, and now we know you're a Jerusalem land buyer!"

I raised my fist to strike back, but the guards rushed in and pinned my arms to my sides.

"Call the British authorities," I demanded.

The sheik laughed. "We *Maraghi* have our own law."

Maraghi! The *Maraghi*, an all-Moslem terroristic brotherhood, were behind every important nationalistic movement of the Arab world. Fearless and fanatic, their influence spread from Iran to Morocco. The *Maraghi* were dangerous; their organization was secret, and often their most potent weapon was not argument or propaganda but cold-blooded assassination.

Their leader was an itinerant preacher in constant flight from the French and British. Sheik Ayatollah Sayed Kashani, popularly known as the Sheik of Fire, was courageous, highly intelligent, and had the ability to recruit followers wherever he went. As we know today, Kashani was for years the power behind Iranian Premier Mohammed Mossadegh. He was also the man, so it was said, who exerted the greatest influence upon the *Grand Mufti* of Jerusalem; and he advised Sultan Abdul Krim of Morocco. Kashani and his movement were a potent danger for practically every existing government of the Middle East.

I knew Kashani had a handful of followers in Palestine and Syria, but I never thought I would be threatened by one of them.

From the expression on her face, I knew that Arana was in terror of the sheik, who now stood revealed as the real master of the village. If I got no help from outside, I was finished.

I was led across the village to the mosque. There in one of the rooms the guards opened a trapdoor, and pushing me down a short flight of steps, slammed the trap door shut, and left me in total darkness. Furious and feeling a little ridiculous, I stood there and cursed the sheik in every language I knew.

Gradually my anger subsided, and I could be somewhat more objective about my position. Why, I asked myself, hadn't I listened more carefully to those who had warned me about making one-man expeditions into hostile Arab districts?

My cell was small, about four feet by four, with a ceiling of barely six feet and walls of very damp rock. I could only stand, to sit was uncomfortable. The airless space quickly became stuffy and unbearably hot, and I started to panic. I stifled an urge to shout; there were no friendly ears to hear.

In the darkness I lost track of time. I could hear the ticking of my wristwatch but couldn't see its face. Counting the seconds, I tried marshaling them into minutes, but soon it was all confusion, and my bewilderment became hysteria. I tapped along the walls in search of an exit, but the walls were solid, a fact that paradoxically brought me a moment's relief. Once again I began to tick off the seconds, and counted more than a thousand before falling asleep on the floor of my dank prison.

Footsteps from the floor above awakened me. The bolt slid on the trap door; the door opened, sending down a welcome flood of moonlight. Arana beckoned me upward with her finger to her lips.

There was a basket at her feet and I opened it hungrily. The smell of hot coffee permeated the room, and ravenously I drank the coffee and bolted down the bread and scraps of goat cheese. After I had finished eating, Arana led me through the open door to the courtyard, where two men waited near the trees. I breathed the cool night air and saw the stars brilliant above me in the cloudless sky.

"Go with these men," she said. "Hurry!"

I had scant time to thank her. Quickly and quietly we passed through the village to the outskirts where donkeys were waiting. To the back of one were tied my knapsack and sleeping bag. We mounted and hurried along the back road, soon leaving it to cut across the fields and foothills.

For more than an hour my companions, their faces hidden by their *gallabiyyas*, were silent. Finally one of them muttered a direction, and I recognized the *muktar's* voice.

He came to my side when we had reached a road obviously well traveled in the day. "This will take you to Bittir," the *muktar* said.

"Your sheik," I said, "won't he know you set me free?"

"He will, but he cannot prove it. Your escape will make it possible for us to accuse him of negligence, and we will demand that the *Grand Mufti* in Jerusalem remove him from our village." The *muktar's* voice rose in anger. "He is a man of hate and has brought blood to our streets. He twists the Koran to suit his own purposes. We don't want him in Der el-Sheik."

He handed me a basket. "This is from my mother. And remember — don't stop until you're safe in Jerusalem."

The *muktar* and his companion turned and disappeared into the night. I set off down the road, and it was morning when I arrived in Bittir. I sold the donkey to the first merchant I saw, and caught the early bus to the city.

When I arrived at my home, my wife was eager to hear about the trip, but I was too exhausted to speak. I stumbled to the shower and then fell on the bed. I needed sleep; days and nights of sleep. As I closed my eyes, Sonja asked from the other room if I had found anything of interest.

"There are some shards in my knapsack," I managed to say before drifting off.

Sonja awoke me in the evening, insisting that I have something to eat. Over the coffee she said, "Where did you find those things in your knapsack?"

"Just some shards. They stopped me from digging just when I thought I was coming to something."

"But what about the face and that snake?"

"You're joking."

She brought in the knapsack and took out the coiled sandstone snake, covered with the patina of centuries, and the mask of sunbaked clay. I realized that the mask was undoubtedly of prepatriarchal days, and both objects have since been definitely established as of Sumerian origin. But the snake — after Arana's story about the snake-devil Affrit — was particularly exciting. It has been displayed at the New York Metropolitan Museum and elsewhere as part of an exhibit titled "The Land of the Bible."

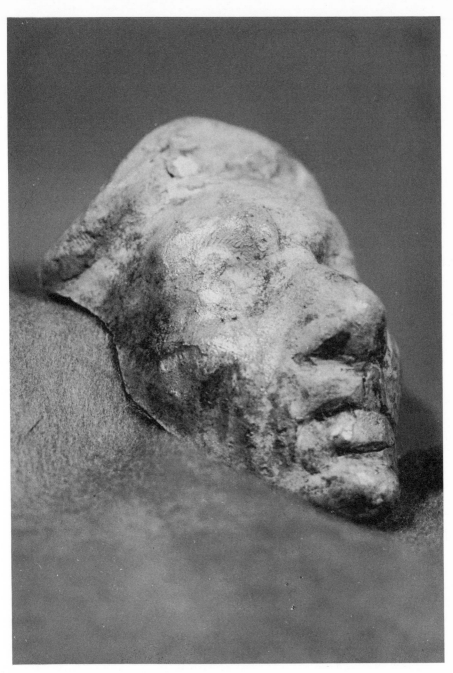

Sumerian mask, 3″ long.

The kindness and understanding of Arana had turned an otherwise fruitless trip into an important archaeological occasion.

2

The ivory plaque fragment and the lotus leaf were the results of an earthquake. As a matter of fact, I wasn't even on an archaeological hunt when I found them. I had promised my wife to avoid for a while any dangerous forays into the Arab hinterland, and Sonja was pleased when one of my newspapers gave me an assignment in Damascus, to interview the leading French and Arab statesmen. It was a hot afternoon in late September when I finished my Syrian assignment, and this time I had small inclination to go on an archaeological expedition. I wanted to be in Jerusalem, sitting on the porch with my wife and my friends, enjoying the local air conditioning of the Moabite breezes. The Damascan heat dissuaded me from the gritty train ride to Jerusalem, and I decided instead to hire a car for the journey home. The friendly hotel manager found a car and driver for me, and at six the next morning a grinning Arab boy in a battered Chevrolet pulled up at the hotel entrance.

Abdul, I soon discovered, had only recently learned to drive a car; his elementary knowledge included an ability to start, steer, and stop. He had been a cameleer, the profession of his father and forefathers, and had accepted the evolution from camel to automobile as naïvely as his family had accepted the displacement of the kerosene lamp by electric light. Had Abdul, instead of adopting the profession of chauffeur, taken a job at one of the new factories springing up around the larger cities, he would have learned to operate his machine with a fair degree of competence. But had it broken down, he would have been as unconcerned as he was helpless to repair it. The same was true of his car; it was the European and the American who knew and cared about such things. Who could be moved by the health or sickness of an engine or a machine?

Abdul raced along the primitive highway like a grinning madman, stretching a long plume of dust behind us. By eight o'clock we had reached the frontier of Syria and Palestine at Rosh Pinna. I told Abdul that if the car held up we would have breakfast in Tiberias, coffee in Nazareth, lunch in Nablus, and dinner in Jerusalem. I promised him baksheesh if he could hold to schedule.

Abdul chattered on about himself and his family, sparing me no details about his siblings, cousins, and aunts. As it happens often with complete strangers, I was learning more about him than I knew of people who had been my acquaintances for years. When we had run out of family anecdotes, Abdul sang old Arabic folk songs in a thin but pleasant voice. We breakfasted in Tiberias; off we rattled toward Nazareth.

In Nazareth we had refreshments and started off again. The sky was a brilliant blue; a cooling breeze came from the distant desert. The road both before and behind us was empty of other cars, though we passed an infrequent Arab bus, its passengers silent and stoical like figures in a wax museum.

I told Abdul about the Hotel Falistine in Nablus where we would stop for lunch. Glancing at my watch I saw it was a little after ten; we should easily reach Nablus before noon.

Slowly we mounted upward into the Judean mountains. We were only six or seven miles from Nablus, whose outlying suburbs I could see on the horizon, when I had a sensation as of an express train passing beneath us. Abdul abruptly pressed down hard on the brake. Before I could protest, he grabbed me by the arm, opened the door, and pulled me out of the car.

"Into the fields!" he shouted, "Into the fields!" I was too stunned to disobey. A hundred yards from the road his grip loosened, and breathing heavily, he sank to his haunches in the dry loam. He bowed his head, and began to pray.

I was sure the boy had gone insane. What was I to do? The nearest Arab village was at least two miles away; the road was deserted. Abdul's car stood with doors open, a symbol of madness, in its center.

Suddenly I heard the distraught bellow of a distant cow. It was answered by another animal cry of fear, then another. There was a rising clamor of bovinity in distress. I had never heard so frightening a sound.

I looked up into the sky that had been so serene and clear a moment before. Now it was gray and lowering. Several miles away a thin plume of dust rose from the ground. The nearby olive trees, bushes, and shrubs came alive with the deafening chatter of birds in the hundreds. Then, as though by signal, the birds flew into the air, darting crazily in all directions as though blown aimlessly by an unseen storm. The sun was hidden by mountains of yellow-gray dust that were rushing toward us; by now the sky had darkened perceptibly, as if in a matter of seconds night had overtaken day.

Blind to the holocaust that swept toward us, Abdul crouched at his prayers. I turned to another unfamiliar sound, high and keening, like the cry of panic-stricken children. It came from the throats of hundreds of jackals that, flushed from their lairs, raced toward the hills. I was unable to breathe the thick, dust-laden air and felt suffocated. I bent to my knees next to Abdul in a spasm of coughing.

Under me the express train roared again, this time much more loudly. The earth trembled and shook; then, as if the train had met in head-on collision with another, there was a terrific rending crash. I was knocked off my feet; Abdul was lifted three or four feet in the air.

I crawled to him where he lay motionless but evidently unhurt among the furrows. We waited for another tremor but it did not come, and cautiously I got to my feet and looked about me. We were surrounded by climbing pillars of dust and earth; great fissures had appeared in the ground around us. I began to shake from shock, and the boy gently put his arm around my shoulder. His color had returned; he was himself again.

"Come," he said comfortingly, "let us go to Nablus. Perhaps we can be of help there."

As we went toward the car I could see smoke from the fires in Nablus. Around us were crevices made by the earthquake; we had to jump several. Directly behind the car was a four-yard ditch in the road. Ahead the road appeared passable, though we would have to proceed slowly and with caution.

Three miles before Nablus the road became impassable and we were obliged to abandon the car. As we entered the outskirts of the town, debris blocked the streets before us. On all sides buildings had collapsed in fire and rubble. Through the smoke and flame we could see the stunned townspeople stumbling awkwardly among the bodies of the dead. New blazes erupted constantly. I saw frantic men clawing at the bricks and fallen walls that had buried their wives and children. Mothers called for lost infants; children screamed in panic. From one house a woman ran holding the body of a child charred from burns. Everywhere we heard the moans of the injured.

Abdul and I did what we could, helping to carry the wounded to the fields outside the town where tents had been put up quickly. Until medical personnel and supplies arrived from Jerusalem we could accomplish little for the burned and injured, and we joined the group of men hunting among the rubble for the dead and missing.

The Hotel Falistine had been destroyed completely. Twelve had died in the dining room where I had planned to lunch that fatal noon hour. The Arab owners and many of the British living at the hotel had been killed outright.

For three days I stayed in Nablus, working with the rescue squads, sleeping four hours a night in one of the flimsy tents. When Abdul and I were discharged, he went to Nazareth, where British soldiers had brought his car, and from there to Damascus. Before he left I offered him payment which he refused, saying, "It was Allah's wish that I save you, and in doing His will I have reward enough."

There were tears in my eyes as I pressed his hand in thanks.

The boy's simple words had touched me. I was ashamed that I could not approach the oneness and trust a naïve boy such as Abdul had with his God. The Moslem had blind but utter faith in all the things God vouchsafed to his children; in Abdul's case, his car and the unshaded electric light that swung from the ceiling of his house in the compound. They and all the appurtenances of his life would do their job with no effort from him. Allah would provide and protect; he need have no fear, but only listen to his word and hew to his law. Perhaps the faith of a simple Arab like Abdul was as meaningful in the final sum of things as that of a great man like Munim. It was fitting, as I later realized, that among many people and many nations I had seen religion; but only in the land of the Bible had I witnessed pure and unquestioning faith.

My truck transportation to Jerusalem was not scheduled to leave until early the morning after next, and having another day and night in Nablus, I decided to visit the site of a former excavation in nearby Sebaste.

Only recently I had read the then unpublished account of J. W. Crowfoot's excavation of Israelite ruins in Samaria, now Sebaste. Crowfoot had unearthed there nine ivory plaques representing mythological Babylonian animals and gods, along with other plaques of Egyptian design that clearly indicated foreign influence in the time of Ahab and his ill-famed wife, Jezebel.

Crowfoot's plaques had fascinated me, upholding as they did the historicity of the Biblical stories that centered around Sebaste, a small Arab village in the mountains of Ephraim, once part of the ancient province of Samaria. The excavated ruins of Sebaste had revealed four distinct cities. In the first level had been unearthed the royal capital of the province, once the center of an independent and flourishing kingdom of Biblical times. The second level had shown a city plainly an administrative headquarters of the Assyrian empire, while in the third archaeologists had discovered buildings patently Roman in architecture and decoration. The fourth level had shown evidence of the Roman Empire's dissolution and its replacement by some kind of autonomous colonial authority under the aegis of various medieval Arab potentates.

Antedating Biblical Samaria, evidence had been found that as early as the Bronze Age, from 3000 to 2000 B.C., the rocky summits of the Ephraim mountains had been inhabited by a primitive people. But it was not before the beginning of the ninth century B.C. that the hills of

Sebaste had attracted permanent settlement. Babylonia had ruled here and so had the Egyptians. It was after the death of Solomon that Sebaste had entered into Biblical history. Omri, sixth king of Israel, paid two talents of silver to Shemer, a landowner, for four hills in the vicinity now known as Sebaste and built the town of Shemer, which later became known as Samaria.

This event is recounted in I Kings (16:23-24, *RSV*): "In the thirty-first year of Asa king of Judah, Omri began to reign over Israel, and reigned for twelve years: six years he reigned in Tirzah. He bought the hill of Samaria from Shemer for two talents of silver; and he fortified the hill, and called the name of the city which he built, Samaria, after the name of Shemer, the owner of the hill."

The Crowfoot excavations in Samaria had established the hill of Shemer as a prominent landmark in early Biblical times. Shemer then commanded two main routes from the south and east, and in the mind of Omri these had outweighed the lack of a natural water supply. Shemer had a prominent citadel and a lower town. The huge square stones of its walls testify today to the strength of the citadel, though nothing is left of the buildings inside it, among which we may surmise the royal palace was one.

It was here, according to I Kings (22:39), that a two-story building was erected, later notorious among Hebrew scholars and priests as the "ivory house" where Jezebel conducted her affairs. No specific remains of this "ivory house" had been found, but it was in a heap of rocks covering the royal chambers that Crowfoot had found his ivory plaques. Equally unidentified was the temple built by Jezebel in commemoration of Baal. But both Crowfoot's and an earlier Harvard expedition to Sebaste had unearthed pottery shards with Hebrew writing telling of events that had taken place in the town. Nearly seventy such shards had been discovered in a ruined building near the Israelite citadel; among them invoices, private messages, and a letter written by an employer to his agent. Some of these included names corresponding with similar names mentioned in I and II Kings.

Crowfoot had made another confirmation of the Bible when he came across a plastered reservoir noted in I Kings (22:38) as the pool of Samaria, where Ahab's chariot was washed after the fatal battle of Ramoth-gilead, in which Ahab was killed in his ill-advised attempt to defeat the king of Aram. No other part of the Holy Land had been so lavish in its confirmation of the Book of Books as Sebaste-Samaria.

As I walked to the site, I recalled that once before in modern times earthquakes had partially destroyed the city. In the old citadel the recent damage was extensive. The ancient stones were rent with deep fissures; marble columns had toppled over; many of the walls and floors carefully uncovered by archaeologists were broken or damaged.

I made my way carefully among the debris and crevices, but my foot was caught suddenly in the tapering end of a wide crevice, and bending down to extricate my foot, I saw, with the help of my flashlight, what appeared to be a small chamber in the ground below. In a distant corner of the chamber two objects gleamed — one white, one golden. I freed my foot and looked for a handhold that would permit me to climb down into the chamber. Finding one, I had begun to clamber down when I heard someone shout: "Don't go in there! It is forbidden!"

I ignored the warning and continued, dirt from the ground above raining down my neck in a steady stream. Finally I made my way close enough to the bottom to drop the remaining few feet. As I did so, I could hear an excited battle of voices above me. Hunched over in the scanty headroom the sloping ceiling afforded me, I was making my way toward the objects in the corner when, with the sound of a heavy sigh, the ceiling collapsed upon me. I was thrown face downward and felt an unbearable pain in my left shoulder. The last thing I remember was reaching forward to grasp the two objects that lay close together, before rocks, stones, and soil pressed me to the floor.

It took the Arab guard on the site more than an hour to dig me out, and only the lucky way in which I fell, arm bent about my face, prevented me from smothering. My back was badly bruised and there were severe cuts on my left shoulder.

Half unconsciously, half surreptitiously, I had somehow smuggled the objects into my shirt before the Arabs had bandaged my bleeding shoulder. They scolded me for trespassing and entering condemned property, but good-naturedly enough brought me back to my tent in Nablus. The doctor arrived to attend to my wounds and bruises, and when he left I was free to examine my treasures.

Ivory fragment, bottom half of dancer, 3" long.

The first, when I had cleaned off its encrusted dirt, was revealed as a fragment of ivory plaque resembling those of Crowfoot's that I had often admired in the Jerusalem Museum. It was the bottom half of a dancer, exquisitely carved; the dancer's legs were poised delicately in the typically tiptoe manner of Phoenician and Egyptian statues and figurines of the period. The other was a small and perfect lotus leaf of beaten gold, probably part of a throne or wall panel inlay. Historic value of these pieces lay in their further confirmation of Biblical evidence of Egyptian-Phoenician cultural influence among the Hebrews in the time of Ahab and Jezebel. The ivory plaque could, as could Crowfoot's fragments, be pieces from Jezebel's ivory house.

My friends in Jerusalem thought I had been foolish to take such chances after an earthquake, but I could no more have stayed out of that chamber than iron filings can resist a magnet.

3

Finally, the ring of Julia Domna represents the most fantastic stroke of luck of all. Granted that a certain instinct was necessary to know where to search for it, the idea of lifting it from its centuries-old hiding place is fantastic, especially under the circumstances I am going to relate.

Often I had made the town of Tiberias my vacation headquarters. I loved its somnolence, its sense of remoteness in time, as if untouched by history. Many of the town's elderly Arabs and its goldsmiths were my friends. It was here I was able to find real peace and tranquillity; the Sea of Galilee region was the only place in Palestine I had found where a man could *keef. Keef* is an abbreviation of the Arab word *kefak*, meaning a state of good health in which one does absolutely nothing. *Kefak* comes closest in meaning to the Indian nirvana. In Tiberias a man could live "à la *kefak*" to his heart's content.

Whenever time and circumstances permitted I went there to stay either in the German-owned, meticulously clean Tiberias Hotel or as the guest of a Swiss missionary, Lily Wreshner, who strove tirelessly to bring the Gospel to the area's recalcitrant Arabs and Jews. Another western friend in Tiberias was the Very Reverend Samuel Sloan, leader of the small Church of England congregation. Dr. Sloan spoke eleven modern languages, but from among all the lands and cities of the globe he had chosen as his home Palestine, and Tiberias.

Lily, Dr. Sloan, and I often sat on the shore of the Sea of Galilee reminiscing under the blooming oleanders. In the moonlight we could see clearly the eastern and westernmost limits of the Lake called the Sea of Galilee, which is the only sweet-water lake in the Holy Land. To

our left was Capernaum; to our right Kinnereth; and directly opposite
the towering mountains of Jolan, once a rich granary of the kingdom of
Israel. The evenings were so quiet that sometimes we heard the echo of
our conversation. Our talk centered around the past and the events in
the Holy Land that nineteen hundred years ago had formed the philo-
sophical and theological sinews of the modern Christian world. I wondered why the Sea of Galilee district, so rich in these events, had never
truly been archaeologically researched. In the time of Herod, Tiberias
was a city of over a hundred thousand. Population of the province of
Galilee has been estimated as close to one million. Much must have
taken place here never recorded in history.

While many Galilean sites had figured conspicuously in Christ's
work and ministry, very few had been definitely identified. No real
work of excavation had been carried out except at Tell Hum, at the
ruins of the now generally accepted site of Capernaum. Recently the
Jewish Palestine Exploration Society had started work at Khirbet Kerah,
near Kinnereth, where it hoped to find remnants of the old Canaanite
City of the Moon, Beth-yerah. But excavation at the great cave in the
Wadi (valley) el-Amud had been discontinued.

Chief archaeological interest in the Galilee area centers around the
Roman and Judean-Herodian period (47 B.C.–A.D. 30), and the time,
consequently, of the New Testament. There is, however, evidence of
ancient Canaanite or Hebrew settlement that has been unexplored. Discussing this with my Tiberias friends, we began running through the
Galilean sites as described in Old and New Testaments.

The northernmost site of importance on the Sea of Galilee is that
of Chorazin, known today as Khirbet Kerazeh. The ruins of this ancient
New Testament town are not easy to recognize as such, for practically
all the stone and masonry above ground have been carted away for
building purposes by the local Arabs. The Arab village of Tell Hum
(ancient Capernaum) was built shortly before the time of Christ. Ruins
of an old synogogue had been discovered where, according to Mark,

John, Matthew, and Luke, Jesus had preached to the poor of Galilee. It was in Capernaum where the toll house stood and where the tax collectors against whom Christ inveighed resided. Remnants of the ancient ark containing the Torah and of the original floor mosaic have been found in Capernaum. In the latter can be identified pomegranate seeds, arrow heads (the symbol of death), and the symbols of Solomon (grape clusters and palm leaves).

Not far from Capernaum is the hill known as the Mount of Beatitudes, and not far from the Mount are the ruins of the small towns of Dalmanutha and Magdala, birthplace of Mary Magdalene. The modern Arab village of Magdala consists of ten to fifteen primitive clay houses that strongly have the character and atmosphere of Biblical times. Most of the villagers are poor fishermen.

One morning, watching the fishermen of Tiberias mending their nets on the beach, an idea came to me, and I forgot I had come here for a rest. Perhaps some of these men sometimes found relics fishing in the Sea. I approached one of them, a dark and handsome fellow with flashing eyes. His name was Hassan. His nets had never recovered objects of the past but others had. Yes, *Chawadjah*, he was willing to try — for a consideration. We bargained, and I agreed to charter his rowboat for the afternoon.

I turned up at four o'clock, when the air had cooled, to find Hassan ready and waiting. The boat was scrubbed clean, there were two quart bottles of water and lemonade in the stern, and a battered sun hat lay under one of the thwarts. Hassan bowed me aboard, and pressed the hat upon me with a flourish.

"You will need this, *Chawadjah*." His white teeth flashed like a Venetian gondolier's. "I bought it for you especially."

"What else will we need?" I asked, looking around.

"Nets." He pointed to two small nets in the bow. "And also patience."

Hassan shoved off and picked up the oars. For about fifteen minutes Hassan rowed parallel to the shore until he came to a cove, where he shipped the oars and looked admiringly upward. Above us on a slight rise were the shambles of a modern Arab house.

"Why here?" I asked.

He shrugged. "Those are ruins. If you are looking for objects of the past, what better place to look for them than near ruins?"

I laughed. But perhaps he was right; in this improbable treasure hunt one place seemed as likely as another.

Hassan dropped anchor in the shallow water, threw out his cork-edged nets, and inquired if I had a cigarette. I handed him a Player's, the first of many that afternoon.

We waited. It was still hot in the declining sun. I finished half the bottle of lemonade, Hassan the rest. He told me the story of his life. Then we started on the bottle of water.

When two hours had passed I asked Hassan if we shouldn't pull up the nets and, if they were empty, try another spot.

He complied. Except for a few strands of algae the nets were empty. I wiped my perspiring face. "What would you suggest now, Hassan?"

He showed his white teeth. "That is for you to say, *Chawadjah.*"

I was ready to admit that I was a fool and Hassan an arrant opportunist. Briskly I told him to row us back to Tiberias.

He spread his hands wide in mock dismay. "But *Chawadjah,* you have chartered the boat for the entire afternoon! We have been out less than three hours!"

"Why not refund me a portion of my money?"

His smile vanished. He bent to the oars and a few minutes later we were back on Tiberias beach. As I got out of the boat he said, slyly, "Come again, *Chawadjah.*" I heard laughter from his fellow fishermen as I walked up the beach to the hotel.

I told none of my friends of this first disaster, undoubtedly because I fully intended to repeat it if necessary. Sure enough the next morning I was back at the beach, talking to the fishermen; Hassan, fortunately, had gone to Jibrin with his ill-gotten gains. The fishermen listened to me with sober respect, and one answered my question by replying that some years ago a fisherman in the nearby town of Samakh, on the Sea's south corner, had netted a bronze object. My informant laughed, saying the piece this man had found was old and of no value, and in weighting down the net had fooled him into thinking he had made a great catch of fish.

"Can I visit this fisherman of Samakh?" I asked.

The man's reply was discouraging; Aba Shemer, the finder of the bronze object, was old now and retired. He had turned his boat over to his son. I thanked the man and returned to my hotel.

Aba Shemer did not leave my mind. I still had three days of vacation left, and early the next morning I took the rachitic Arab bus to Samakh, an important trading center. The bazaar was always filled with villagers and *fellahin* from miles around. Here they traded their grain, vegetables, and animals. I looked up my old friend Achmed, the *muktar,* and he directed me to the house of the old fisherman. Since he was working no longer the man was known now under the name of Aba, father of Shemer, and he was almost forgotten. When I reached the old man's house on the outskirts of the town, I saw an aged but still powerful *fellah* sitting in the courtyard under a eucalyptus tree. I made the customary salaams out of respect to his years. Then I said I had come to conduct business with him.

"Business?" He looked up at me curiously. "I am retired, *Chawadjah.* I have no fish to sell. I no longer have even a boat."

The honesty of his withered face made me take an immediate liking to him. "I have not come to buy fish," I said. "I know you have retired. But someone has told me that years ago you took from the sea something that was no fish. I have come to see it." I introduced myself then, telling him I was an archaeologist, but evidently the word was unfamiliar to him.

Aba invited me to sit down beside him in the courtyard. After a lengthy discussion, he went into the house and returned holding some bronze implements so badly eroded that at first I was hard put to determine their original use. One I recognized finally as the blade of a short bronze Roman sword. Two others I identified as part of a Roman soldier's or centurion's bronze epaulettes, and half a soldier's belt buckle.

"This, *Chawadjah*, is all I found."

When I opened my coin purse to pay him what I thought the pieces were worth, Aba looked at me in astonishment. But he accepted the silver coins gratefully.

"If you will take me to the place where these were found," I told him, "I will pay you well."

"That I cannot do," the old man said. "I have promised my sons never to go fishing again."

I emptied my coin purse into his hand.

He smiled broadly. "Well, *Achuya* (my brother), I should at least listen carefully to what you have to say." He clapped his hands, and as if conjured out of thin air, a beautiful, unveiled young girl appeared from the house, and waited respectfully.

"Your youngest daughter?" I asked.

"Aiya, my wife."

Aiya couldn't have been more than eighteen years old, and the old man was approaching eighty. I tried to hide my astonishment, and looked at the two pleasantly as if such a marriage were an everyday occurrence. I couldn't help pitying the girl, but I soon saw I was mistaken; examining her more closely, I saw she was in her fifth or sixth month of pregnancy.

Aiya disappeared into the house to make us coffee, emerging a few moments later with a long-handled coffee pot and two small cups. Gracefully she served us. She was a beautiful girl, and I was sure Aba would do anything within reason to make her happy.

I had an idea. Perhaps if I promised the old man a costly gift for Aiya he would go along with me. I told him the goldsmith in Tiberias had made silver bracelets and ankle rings for the nobility, and that I could easily buy some of these for his lovely young wife. Aba didn't answer me immediately, but I sensed I had found his weak point.

Aiya came to pour us a second cup, and from the way Aba's eyes lingered on her arms and ankles, I knew I had won my case.

"*Achuya,*" he said, "you have made it impossible for me to refuse. But we must cast the nets at night. I will borrow a rowboat and meet you a mile from the village, for none of my sons must see me fishing again."

For the next half-hour we discussed our plan, and arranged to meet two nights later at ten o'clock at a spot on the shore he described in detail to me. I left for Tiberias.

There in my hotel room I examined the four bronze objects. My first hasty identification had been correct. All were part of a Roman officer's equipment. The richly decorated epaulette was surely that of a captain or centurion.

It was difficult for me to determine exactly what period the pieces were from. Many battles had been fought on the shores of the Sea of Galilee. Roman garrisons had been established in Tiberias and other towns on or near the Sea in the time of Herod the Great and Herod Antipas. Prior to the Roman conquest of Jerusalem in A.D. 70 the Jews and Romans had been constantly at one another's throats. Here Flavius Josephus, later to turn renegade, had fought unsuccessfully against the army of Vespasian. The Hebrew Zealots had been furious fighters, and much Roman blood had flowed into the waters of the Sea.

What had begun as mostly a lark became now in my mind a significant scientific endeavor. The next morning I selected two heavily embossed silver bracelets and a finely engraved anklet in the goldsmith's shop, paying the price of two very fine dinners.

That evening I showed the bronze objects to my friends Lily Wreshner and Dr. Sloan. Sloan was not surprised to learn they had been fished up from the bottom of the Sea. To his knowledge many such ancient objects had been discovered near Tiberias from time to time. Six years before, part of a crusader's chain mail had been found and sent to a museum in Edinburgh, Scotland.

Later that night I pored over the history books in my hotel room. I had been so involved with the time of Christ that I had forgotten much of what had transpired here in other periods. After the fall of Jerusalem (A.D. 70) the Romans had occupied Palestine for another three hundred fifty years, and not far from Samakh, where Bab lived, Greek and Roman religious life had played a large part in the cultural life of the inhabitants. I had forgotten the once large and important Roman fortress and agricultural town of Gadara on the slopes of the mountains of Gilead, where the Roman emperor Septimus Severus had sent his Syrian wife, Julia Domna, to exile.

All the next day I restlessly paced the beach and hotel lobby, too keyed-up to read or meet with my friends. Shortly before sundown I took the bus to Samakh and spent the hours till darkness in the Arabic restaurant; how many plates of *lahme shaf* (broiled lamb) I ate I do not know. At nine o'clock I made my way to the meeting place. Aba had not yet arrived. Through the tall reeds I could see a rowboat drawn up on the beach.

Suddenly the whole venture seemed utterly ridiculous, and my spirits fell. Hassan had failed me; how could I expect any better of Aba? How could I be sure there were other objects where he had found the Roman military accoutrements six years before; or, if others had at one time been there, the tides and currents had not moved or buried them beyond removal in the bottom mud? Perhaps it wasn't too late to return to Samakh and Tiberias, resell the jewelry, and go back to Jerusalem to take up my more sensible work.

Then I heard shuffling footsteps, and a moment later Aba was at my side. He salaamed and said, "A perfect night for fishing."

I helped him to unfold the huge net which, he told me, would cover an area of twenty square yards on the bottom of the sea. We clambered into the rowboat, and Aba rowed slowly toward the middle of the Sea, about a mile distant. I was amazed at the old man's strength; he rowed the heavy boat with regular, powerful strokes and without interruption. It must have been shortly before eleven when the blue-silver moon rose over the mountains, changing the color of the sea from black to a ghostly bluish white. We could see the shore and the hills and the tall minarets of the mosques in Tiberias and Samakh.

Aba shipped his oars and threw out the leaden weight that served as an anchor. "Here is the place, *Chawadjah*. Help me throw out the net."

The net touched bottom and we saw the corks bobbing on the water. "We must wait now," said Aba. "One hour, two, perhaps till sunrise. The constant undercurrent, if we are fortunate, will sweep whatever objects there are near here into the net. When we are ready I will tell you."

He took his prayer beads from his pocket and began to count them silently. The beads were on a string, like a rosary, and each bead represented a *sura* (chapter) of the Koran. I was reluctant to interrupt the old man, but of his own accord he began to tell me of his life as a fisherman, of the times when he had had big catches and enough money for his three wives and fourteen children, and of the times when the catch was small, and he had had a hard time providing food for his family.

"Are all your sons fishermen, and your daughters married?" I asked him.

"Only the two eldest sons of my first wife are fishermen. Two other boys joined the British police, and three are carpenters. The girls are all married. They were handsome, and their husbands paid me well." He paused. "Two of my children drowned during a stormy night at sea."

"I am sorry to hear it."

"Do not be sorry, *Chawadjah*. Their deaths were Allah's will, and against Allah's will man is powerless."

I counted the hours by the position of the moon. Two hours passed, then a third. I grew more and more impatient; Aba's tales of his father and grandfather, fishermen before him, had long since ceased to amuse me.

"Is it time to pull in the net?" I asked.

"Not yet, *Chawadjah*."

"Why not?"

"Everything has its given time," he answered philosophically, and sighing, I returned to my vigil. Finally I said, "I have the silver jewelry for your wife."

A happy smile crossed his face.

"She is very lovely," I said.

"Yes," Aba said, "and she is young. She comes from the mountains," he said, and pointed to the east, toward Syria. "Her father is a farmer who was punished by Allah in having only girl children. She did not cost me much, and she is devoted and faithful." The old man closed his eyes, and it seemed as though he had fallen asleep.

I must have dozed myself; suddenly I heard Aba saying, "It is time now, *Chawadjah*."

I opened my eyes to the beginning of a new day. To the east, over the mountains, the sky was brightening. We began to pull in the net.

"Look to the bottom of the net as we pull it in, a little at a time," said Aba. "If we have found anything, it will be there in the mud."

The net was heavy with fish. True to his promise to his sons, Aba threw them back into the sea one by one, and I was free to examine the netting. I found nothing, and grew more and more reluctant in my search. But then my fingers came in contact with something hard. It was the fragment of a sword blade, and I examined the algae more carefully.

Practically the entire net had been hauled into the boat when I encountered something small, hard, and round. The sensation was as if my fingers had touched glass. I washed the mud-encrusted object in the water and held it up to the first rays of the rising sun.

In my hand lay a silver ring, the metal badly corroded, but still in its original form. Engraved in intaglio on a carnelian stone was a face of Julia Domna, the exiled wife of the Roman emperor Septimus Severus. Seventeen hundred years before, she had been a prisoner in the fortress of Gadara, in the mountains some miles from the Sea.

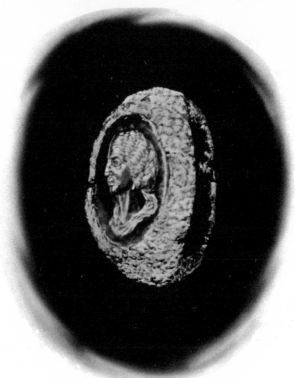

Ring of Julia Domna, 1¼″ oval.

"What do you have there, *Chawadjah?*" asked Aba.

"An ancient ring of great value. Aba, you have earned this night much more than my gratitude."

Aba looked at the ring and shrugged. It was incredible to him that such an object could be of importance, but he was used to the Westerner's whims, which were sometimes profitable.

When I returned to Jerusalem the next day, I showed the ring to Sukenik and Olaf Madson. They confirmed it as the original sealstone ring, worn probably on a chain around her neck, and the only badge of office remaining to her from the great and lavish past of the Syrian princess who became a Roman Empress and the mother of Geta and Caracalla.

PART THREE

» VIII «

The Mate of the Lotus Flower

IN MY collection there are several objects that recall stories that beg to be told. And, too, a life of archaeology is certain to result in many adventures that prove completely unrewarding as scientific projects, but are priceless as human experience. In this part of the book I have gathered several of my best stories although, as I have said earlier, they do not belong under the title of this book in the strictest sense. The objects or experiences have no real Biblical significance. But as sidelights on a career in archaeology I hope you will find them as interesting as I did when they happened to me.

For example, during the many years I spent in Jerusalem, Hebron, and Damascus I was always attracted to the small and cluttered goldsmith shops, where skilled craftsmen plied an ancient trade. It was to the goldsmith that the Arab farmer brought for sale or for melting down unfamiliar objects found by him. The *fellahin* trusted the integrity of the goldsmith, and in my travels and wandering through the land of the Bible, I learned to trust him too.

Most of the native goldsmiths knew me and what I searched for, though sometimes they were ignorant of the archaeologist and his work. Such was the case in the little village of Aquarra, near Tulkaram. Tulkaram is the agricultural center of the southern plains of Palestine, and Aquarra is famous for its watermelons. When I entered the gold-smith's shop at Aquarra on a day in June I was making merely a routine visit, and my tone was casual as I asked the goldsmith if he had come across any antiquities. He looked at me in a puzzled way, and I saw he did not understand my question. I sat down on an empty kerosene can in the tiny shop and explained more fully.

He shook his head. "No, *Chawadjah,* I have come across nothing worth your while."

He was a busy man. The kerosene-drenched charcoal fire blazed under the melting pot; the smith's foot was on the pedal of his bellows. His left hand was clenched into a fist. Obviously he was holding whatever he planned to melt. I glanced around the shop, looking for something that might interest me, but there was only the usual modern Arabic jewelry.

As he relaxed his grip briefly on the object he was about to melt, I saw the glimmer of gold between his fingers.

"What's in your hand?" I asked.

"A broken earring. A villager is having it melted down into a brace-let. It's a present for his third wife."

I asked to see it, and when he dropped it into my hand I saw that it was an exquisite piece of Egyptian jewelry at least three thousand years old. Its inlay of enamel was deteriorated; the socket adjoining the hook must once have held an emerald, but now it was empty. I was certain of the earring's Egyptian origin, but how it had found its way to the workshop of a goldsmith in Aquarra was a mystery. The earring, curiously enough, looked familiar to me; I was sure this was not the first time I had seen it.

"I'll buy this from you," I said, putting my wallet on the table to show I had money.

"You cannot," he said. "It belongs to the villager."

"You will not melt this down," I said angrily. "You will weigh it, and I will pay you the equivalent in cash. Then you can make a bracelet in new gold for your customer."

Lotus flower gold earring, 2¼" long.

Lotus leaf of beaten gold, 1¾" long.

The old man agreed; he knew I would pay him a sum in excess of the gold's value. When our transaction was complete I asked the smith the name of the Arab who had given him the earring. Minutes later I was in the *fellah's* courtyard.

Here I heard a fantastic story. The Arab had received the earring as an heirloom from his father, who some thirty-five years ago had found it while excavating with an English archaeologist in the Sharon Valley, some twenty miles from Aquarra. In 1894, Duncan McAllister had found there ruins of an Egyptian house dating back to the fourteenth or fifteenth dynasty. Among the objects McAllister had discovered was a gold pendant in the shape of a lotus flower, which he had sent to the British Museum. I remembered now I had seen it in one of the old Museum catalogues.

The father of the Aquarra Arab had found the mate of this earring, but McAllister had not known it existed. After forty years his son had given the earring to the goldsmith to melt down into a bracelet for his newly wed third wife. This was the modern case history of my lotus flower earring, important as one of the few golden antiquities to be found in Palestine.

» IX «

The Mummy Who Rose from the Dead

ALLAN G. SMITH was an unusual and eccentric man. A leading scholar in Egyptology with a world-wide reputation in scarabs and mummification, he was loosely attached to Cairo's Egyptian Museum. We had met some years before when Smith was doing Biblical research in Jerusalem, and several times I had accompanied him on expeditions into upper Egypt. To work with Allan was exciting, for the interpretations he gave to his findings were original and unique, and he reached conclusions — often correct ones — that were widely at variance with those of his colleagues.

I had seen him twice in the past two years. Once he had asked my presence in Alexandria to act as witness in the marriage between one of his servants, a seventy-seven-year-old gardener, and a fourteen-year-old peasant girl. His theory was that males were greatly superior, both physically and mentally, to females, and this marriage was to prove his point. It failed: on her wedding day the young bride ran away with an eighteen-year-old boy. Chagrined, Allan sent away the guests and spent the evening with me in his study, reminiscing of his heedless youth and drinking the strong native Syrian arrack by the glassful.

On another occasion he had come to see me in Jerusalem in a considerable state of excitement, with a find he had just made of great historical importance — hieroglyphic papyrus writing from the time of Pharaoh Amenhotep IV. He wanted to decipher his papyrus in the quietness Jerusalem afforded, and worked for days and nights, only to conclude that the papyrus was no more than a thirty-year-old hoax, expertly executed and aged in the workshop of one of Cairo's more unscrupulous antique dealers.

If I was disappointed, Allan was not. He was all good cheer as I accompanied him to the railway station. Later I found out the reason why. He had ordered three more sets of the false documents and sent them to various friends at English and American universities, asking for their opinions on the documental validity. I don't know how long his colleagues slaved at their own decipherments until they reached their own independent conclusions.

Such a man was Allan Smith — amusing, unpredictable, out of the conventional scholar's mold. Tall, graceful, with alertly inquisitive blue eyes, he was a born adventurer with more than a touch of a zany Sherlock Holmes in him. But he was also a true-born Englishman and a snob, and one thing he had never learned was how to deal with the Arabs. Always polite, reserved, and courteous, he would never stoop to their level; as a superior Anglo-Saxon he looked down his hawklike nose — the nose he was so proud of as a sign of nobility — at the children of Ishmael. Satiric and fastidious and proud of his caste, it was hard for him to make friends, but those he did make were devoted to him.

The telegram he had sent me was from Aswan, in upper Egypt. It said he had discovered, in the village of Ed-Derdah, a tomb from the 11th Dynasty, about 2000 B.C., and that he needed my assistance. I suspected that Allan needed me not only for excavation, but because he was in some kind of difficulty. It was hard for me at the moment to get away from my work in Jerusalem, but when Allan Smith sent me an SOS from the desert, I felt I must respond.

Also, I was excited by his discovery; for any archaeologist, the finding of a tomb from the 11th Dynasty was of great historical importance. The 11th Dynasty was in the general period of the first patriarch, and very little was known of Abraham's time. The Biblical accounts of his sojourn in Canaan and Egypt are slight and often contradictory. Any new discovery of this period, even in Egypt, might shed new light on the Bible.

Two days later I was on my way. The train brought me from Jerusalem to Cairo, and from Cairo to Aswan. There were no roads from Aswan to Ed-Derdah, and the trip by camel was a good thirty-six hours. The sun was setting when I arrived at the Arab village. The hot sun and fatigue of the camel trip had worn me out completely, and I was glad to see the clay huts of Ed-Derdah.

The children were first to spot me, and going down the dusty village street I was surrounded by a horde of boys and girls begging for baksheesh and sweets. From the windows of the houses the veiled women, only their almond eyes uncovered, regarded me as though I were a visitor from another planet. Men lounged silently in the doorways. Where was Allan, I wondered? Why hadn't the sheik come out to greet me?

"Professor Smith!" I shouted. "Where is he?"

There was no answer. In the very silence there was hostility.

With the pressure of my knees I directed the camel to kneel to permit me to dismount. This was a complicated procedure and took several minutes; despite the villagers' hostility, they began to laugh. Finally my feet were on the ground, but my legs felt like rubber.

"Lead me to the sheik of your village," I demanded.

The lounging men stared at me.

"There is an English professor in your village," I said, feeling sudden anxiety for Allan's safety. "Where is he?"

The *fellahin* looked at me without understanding, but my Arabic was fluent enough, and the situation suddenly struck me as a curious one.

Finally one of the loungers detached himself, and scowling, bid me accompany him. A moment later I stood before the sheik Murah-el-Din, a powerful man in his sixties. The courtyard was crowded with his children. Murah did not smile, and his animosity was obvious. This was a man who ruled his village with the authority of a medieval despot. He was the law, and on behalf of his people he resented the intruder.

Politely I asked where I might find Allan. Murah pointed toward the end of the courtyard's outer wall, and there I saw the top of a small British field tent. "He is there," Murah said, "and my prisoner." As I ran to the tent I heard the laughter of the children behind me.

Two scimitar-armed Arabs stood guard before the tent. I turned and looked at the sheik, who nodded. The guards pulled aside the flaps and I went inside, to find Allan sitting on a stool before a small table.

"Hullo, Paul," he said calmly, "did you bring any money?"

"No," I said. "For God's sake, tell me what happened."

He rose, and in his casual manner reached for my hand and pressed it. Then he sat down again. "I'm glad you came," he said. "Sit down."

I took the second stool and sat there, looking at this prototype of the always unperturbed Englishman. His next words made me laugh. "Excuse my not being shaven," he said. "The dictator of this village has appropriated not only my revolver, but my razor, too."

He gestured toward one of the two field cots. "You must be tired. Rest. Never discuss problems when you're out on your feet; I'll tell you what's happened at dinner time. The food, incidentally, is quite adequate here."

I fell on the cot and must have slept at least three hours. When I opened my eyes, I couldn't believe them. There was Allan sitting at the table, dressed formally in his dinner jacket with boiled shirt and cummerbund. Allan Smith might be prisoner in a tent in an Arab village in the middle of the desert three hundred fifty miles from Cairo, but like an English gentleman he still insisted upon dressing for dinner. That this dinner would most likely consist of bread, beans, and rice made not the slightest difference. This conservative propriety, I thought, could be either strength or snobbery; I didn't know which. So I began to dress myself, choosing a shirt with which I could wear one of Allan's ties.

I was right about the bread, beans, and rice, but Allan had been correct about their quality, which was more than passable. Allan discussed commonplaces until we got to our coffee, and then he began his story.

"When I was here six months ago, I noticed a sand hill on the outskirts of the village. I made my first preliminary examination, doing no excavation, but going over the soil and the foundation of the sand hill, which I was certain covered heavy rocks, and very possibly an ancient burial place. My calculation was based on historical research, the hill formation, and the village's geographical location. But my real clue was a stone slab I had found near the hill. On the slab was hieroglyphic writing, and deciphered, it read 'King Intef.' "

"Intef," I repeated excitedly. "Go on." Intef was the name of the only known king of the 11th Dynasty, a period of which practically nothing had been discovered.

"Murah was away at the time, but his elders seemed perfectly co-operative. They asked the villagers if they had ancient relics to sell, and one of the *fellahin* showed me a scarab with the hieroglyphic signs of *Nebcherure*. This was the best possible luck, because *Nebcherure* are the symbols describing the unification of the upper and lower empire. This unification took place in the 11th Dynasty, so I was even more certain that in excavating the hill I would find additional proof of this great political event that took place near the time of Abraham.

"I bought the scarab and left Ed-Derdah for Alexandria. There I made ready the excavation I started twelve days ago." Allan shook his head. "And here I am, a prisoner of the terrible Murah-el-Din, and so, my dear Paul, are you."

"I would assume so," I said dryly. "But continue."

Allan set his cup down delicately. "Well, Murah was friendly at first when I arrived. But the blighter soon showed the cut of his jib. He said the elders had had no right to encourage my return here without his permission, and would be punished. He demanded an exorbitant sum for the right to excavate. When I told him I had no such kind of money, he waved his arms about and shouted at me. When I pointed out my right to excavate, and proved it with authorization papers from the Egyptian government, the old boy really blew up completely.

"He snatched the papers out of my hand and threw them to the floor. There were no Egyptian tombs in Ed-Derdah. If I unearthed what might be beneath the sand hill I would bring bad luck to the village. Legend had it that in these parts was the tomb of Caliph Hakim, an evil tyrant of centuries past who had refused to accept Mohammed and flouted the Koran. In the days of Murah's forefathers the Caliph Abi Bakr had been sent to kill this man, and did. Who knew if the tomb of Hakim was not in Ed-Derdah? If it was, and the tomb was desecrated by a foreigner, the spirit of the evil Hakim would emerge to bedevil the villagers.

"Against such stupidity I was, of course, powerless. I thought to approach Murah again after he had calmed down a bit, and I stayed on in Ed-Derdah instead of leaving for Alexandria, as I should have done. But things went from bad to worse; Murah and the villagers had come to believe that I was in league with Hakim himself. One evening my tent was attacked and my servant, Aly, was beaten. That was when I sent you my second telegram."

"Second?" I asked. "I got only one."

Allan shrugged philosophically. "Then Murah must have prevented Aly from going to Aswan. Aly's probably a prisoner now in another part of the village. It seems reasonable — I haven't seen him for four days. The second telegram asked you to tell the authorities in Cairo and send gold for Murah, the greedy old cutthroat."

I pondered grimly. Until help arrived from the outside it would be weeks, or even months. Allan and I had told no one we were going to Ed-Derdah; among the fraternity the location of an important expedition was always a jealously guarded secret. No one in Jerusalem, not even my wife, expected me back for three weeks to a month, and our situation was really precarious. After a long discussion we decided that I should approach Murah tomorrow and ask not only for our freedom but for permission to excavate. He might be willing to settle for our release.

Next morning the guards refused to let me leave the tent, but Murah came in response to my summons, surrounded by his hoary village elders. He shook his head definitely in response to my request, and when he spoke it was with anger.

"Already the bad spirit has come among us," he said. "This cursed Englishman has brought misery and bad luck. Three women have gone into labor and produced three worthless females. Girls!" he shouted, "not a single boy! Is this not proof of his devilish intentions?"

Careful not to laugh, I did my best to convince Murah that such talk was only superstition and against Moslem belief. But it was like talking to the deaf, and finally, as if compromising, I told him we would be satisfied to leave the village. Then the wily old Arab showed his true stripe, and with naked greed in his eyes, demanded thirty gold coins in ransom.

Now it was my turn for anger. "This is outrageous!" I said. "You are a thief! Allah will punish you!"

But Murah only shrugged and said, "The loss of three boys is more serious than a ransom of thirty gold coins."

Allan, who had heard the entire conversation through the tent flap, greeted me with a grin; it amused him that he had been the cause of three girl children. The ransom threat he took with aplomb — I suppose no gentleman, to his view, showed concern at the prospect of any fate worse than death by fire at the stake. It took me a while to convince him enough of the seriousness of our plight to offer a suggestion for ending it, but finally he came up with a good one. "Why not," he said, lighting a cigarette, "tell the old boy we'll give him all the gold and precious jewels we find in the tomb?" He winked at me.

"But what assurance have we we'll find any valuables? The tomb may have been robbed."

"We might find valuables," said Allan equably. "If we don't, we can think of something else."

Feeling like a character in a story of Middle Eastern adventure and intrigue, I demanded an audience with Murah-eh-Din. This time we spoke alone in the sheik's courtyard. Murah brushed aside my assurances of Allan's innocence and again demanded ransom, but he listened carefully when I told him of the gold, silver, and precious stones that might be found in the sand hill burial place.

"What are thirty gold coins," I said, "when I can offer you a king's ransom, without fear of redress by the Egyptian authorities? And certainly our offer proves we are only scientists, disinterested in wealth; otherwise I would have asked for half the booty."

Murah ordered coffee for me and sat puffing on his narghile. It was two hours later that we sealed our pact. I had Murah's assurance that we could begin the excavation with the help of seven workers, including Aly, whom Allan had guessed correctly had been caught trying to escape. I agreed that Murah should be present when the tomb was opened, so that there was no possibility of his being cheated.

I left the old man on fairly good terms, and Allan was relieved to hear of my successful talk. Early the next morning, after Allan and Aly's affectionate reunion, we started work. The excavation area as established by Allan was twelve feet long and sixteen feet wide, and the first day we removed a foot of sand from the entire area.

Digging continued for the next four days. At a level of eight feet we had found no traces of the tomb, but the sieve yielded up two small granite chips that fired our enthusiasm tremendously, because we recognized them definitely as fragments from the ancient tools used in tomb construction. The next several days were uneventful, but on the morning of the seventh day our shovels hit hard, smooth rock. It was another half day's work to clear the sand from a rock area of four by five feet.

Carefully Allan and I examined every inch of the rock for marks made by the ancient stone hewers that would indicate the architecture of the tomb itself. After three more days we had freed the entire tomb cover, and began digging down the sides to discover the entrance. To save work and time we had to rely upon our intuition, knowing that the tomb entrance could be on only one of the four sides.

Our guess was right, and we found the petrified mortar linking the cover with the tomb entrance. Working again with pick and shovel, we freed the entrance after another forty-eight hours of labor. To our surprise and disappointment, we discovered the ancient seal to be broken; the tomb had been opened by grave robbers perhaps fifty to a hundred years after it had been built. The chances were that all gold and valuables had been removed, something that would amuse Murah little.

Our only course now was to delay the opening of the tomb as long as possible, and to dispatch a wire to one of my friends in Jerusalem asking that he get in touch with Egyptian authorities in Cairo. The plan was for Aly to attempt another escape to Aswan at the earliest opportunity.

As it turned out, opening the tomb was no easy task. The stone slab entrance weighed at least a ton, and without modern machinery was extremely difficult to remove. We chipped away at the mortar and chiseled at the opening carefully, keeping it small so the fresh hot air rushing into the tomb would not destroy what wooden materials were inside; upon contact with fresh, hot air, centuries-old wood often crumbled to dust. When the opening was a foot and a half by three we covered it with cloth. Air escaping from the tomb was ice cold, and we heard a hissing sound as it mingled with the heat of the day.

Our greatest expectations had already dimmed; the tomb, if it consisted of a single chamber, as it most likely did, was much too narrow for a royal burial place. The person buried here could only have been a beloved servant or high official of one of the 11th Dynasty Pharaohs. Even if the tomb had not been ransacked, it was improbable that any unusual valuables would be found. But historically speaking, discovery of the tomb was still an important one.

So far Aly had had no chance to make his escape with our message to the outside world, and Murah's patience was wearing thin. There had been grumblings from the village elders about the white man's "desecration," and feeling about the three girl children still ran high. But finally the tomb opening was large enough for entrance, and that day I informed Murah that by a few hours after sundown the "gold and riches" would be his.

Measuring the temperature every ten minutes, we waited till the heat of the day had cooled. During the day temperatures in the desert valleys of Egypt reach an average of 110 degrees, but after sundown the temperature sinks very rapidly. Two hours after sundown the thermometer had dropped to 75 degrees. We wanted to effect entrance when it read between 60 and 65 degrees.

At last Allan gave the sign. Murah went forward quickly, but I shouted to him, "Wait! There are snakes and scorpions in the tomb. The Professor and I and two of the helpers will go in first, and then we will call you." Murah obeyed, and slowly, Allan going first, we made our way through the opening. With us we had a single torch, which was half extinguished to minimize the destructive heat. I had said that thirty minutes after we had entered, the sheik and four of the Arab helpers might follow us.

In the torch's flickering light we could make out a huge, sarcophagus-like mummy case in the middle of the narrow room. Next to it stood two alabaster jars, and four smaller vases were scattered about on the floor. All these containers were empty, looted by the grave robbers. On the walls I could see some faded hieroglyphic designs; there were also wall paintings depicting the glorious reign of Pharaoh Intef. The person mummified and entombed here must have been a man; there was no trace of a perfume chest, the typical tomb gift for women. There was also no solar boat, the sign of a person of royal or noble blood.

We examined the outer mummy case made of three-inch-thick clay and bearing the painted designs of the 11th Dynasty. Looking for the case's opening, we were so occupied with our work that I had forgotten the thirty minutes had already passed. *"El-dahab!"* cried Murah from the opening. "The gold — where are the gold and precious jewels?"

"Soon," I shouted back. "We are still investigating."

Allan and I shivered in the ice-cold air. Resuming our examination, we found on the bottom of the mummy case, under an engraving of the *ankh,* the hieroglyphs of the man who had been buried here some four thousand years ago. His name was Reheme, and he had been the first scribe of the Pharaoh's son. Not a man of noble birth, he had been important enough in his time to merit his own tomb.

Allan and I and the two helpers removed the outer mummy case, working cautiously so as not to break the fragile clay. Under it we found another case of wood, with a wooden mask of the scribe fastened to it with two copper nails. On the case in hieroglyphics was the story in brief of Reheme's life.

Absorbed in our work, we had forgotten Murah and his impatience completely. Allan was muttering his hope that once the wooden case was removed we would find hieroglyphic papyruses, scriptures, and scrolls still decipherable after four thousand years. In another hour we had removed the wooden case without once splintering the wood. What confronted us now was another wooden case, its geometrical designs symbolizing the path to be taken to the afterworld by the soul of the dead scribe.

This case was lighter and took less labor to detach, and now we saw the mummy itself in its royal bandages. A gold *ankh* hung on a golden chain fastened to the binding. The head was unwrapped, the bony forehead shining in the torch light. The hair of the mummy's temples was gray; his eyes were closed in the deep-sunken sockets. The lips still had a faint color of red; the cheeks and chin, clean-shaven before mummification, looked like faded yellow parchment. Around the neck hung a necklace of golden beads, lapis lazuli, and emerald stones.

There were tears in Allan's eyes, and it was as if I heard from his closed lips a prayer to God asking forgiveness for disturbing the sleep of the dead. The torches trembled in the hands of the Arab helpers as they stood, staring. Time was stopped; it seemed as though the mummy had the power to wipe out the present and hold us, hypnotized, by the past.

Suddenly one of the helpers screamed. I caught his torch as it fell; involuntarily I followed his finger as it pointed to the mummy. As Allan and I watched in fascination and not a little terror, slowly the mummy's head rose, and then his torso. The golden necklace fell with a clinking sound on his folded hands under their bandages as the mummy assumed, with terrible inevitability, a half-sitting position. From his lips came a kind of groaning. His closed eyes stared.

"Hakim! The ghost of the evil Hakim!" screamed one of the Arab helpers.

Shrieking with fear, the other helper cried, "Allah! Mohammed! Save us!" and ran toward the tomb opening. Outside the sheik and other Arab helpers had fled. I reached out and grasped Allan's hand, and in the silent blackness we made our way from the tomb.

Our respite was a brief one. One moment we were breathing the fresh night air of the desert; the next I felt something sharp and hard graze my cheek. A flung stone. Allan gasped with pain as another stone caught him above the knee. Now we heard the taunts of the villagers, shouting that we had been in league with Satan to release the evil spirit of Hakim from the tomb. Crouching, I looked around for Aly in desperation. I prayed to God he had escaped in the hubbub, unseen by the villagers, to Aswan and the telegraph office. There was the sound of running feet. Then fists pounded against my head and chest. Allan and I fought back as well as we could; a good boxer, Allan knocked down quite a few of our attackers. But we were no match for the crowd of them; soon, our hands bound behind our backs, they were marching us back to the village with blows and curses.

When we awoke the sun was high. Allan and I looked at one another's bound hands ruefully, and laughed. I was well aware that Murah could kill or torture us at will, and Allan knew it too; the first words he said to me were, "Forgive me, Paul. This is a sticky business."

I shrugged. "From now on it all depends on Aly."

"Let's hope he got away in the confusion."

I tried to change the subject. "The mummy," I said, "can you explain it?" I had an explanation of my own, but preferred hearing Allan's first.

"I think so. That tomb's been hermetically sealed for at least four thousand years under tons and tons of sand. Air remaining in the chamber at the time of burial has become thinner and thinner over the centuries, until the oxygen has practically disappeared, and the atmosphere freezer-cold. When we opened the tomb we carefully covered the opening to prevent warm air from getting in. While we worked on the mummy cases the air was still thin and cold, but by the time the mummy itself was uncovered, the atmosphere had become considerably warmed by the torches and by what fresh air had entered the tomb through the opening. In contact with this warm air, the mummy's bandages first contracted and then expanded, forcing it into a sitting position. Is that the way you see it?"

I agreed with Allan in every particular.

After a while I got up, and moving to the tent flap, attempted to open it with my bound hands. A strong arm pushed me back. "Bring us something to eat and drink!" I shouted.

I got no answer, but a few moments later Murah entered the tent with four of his men with daggers at the ready. The sheik scowled at us. "You have brought evil and bad luck to our village," he said. "Your servant has escaped with one of our best camels. I have not yet decided if your lives will be forfeit for the damage you have done, or what punishment you will suffer. But if you wish me to spare you, you must return to the tomb and bring me the gold necklace and *ankh* Mustafa, the helper, has told me of."

"Gladly," I said, trying to be as friendly as I could under the circumstances. I made a manful effort to hide my elation at Aly's escape, and said, "Before we re-enter the tomb the Professor and I must rest. We must eat and drink and regain our strength. How else can we face the spirit of Hakim?"

Allan looked at me as if I were out of my mind, but with my eyes I cautioned silence. The only thing worth fighting for now was time. Murah was agreeable; food and water were brought to us and our bonds untied. I tried to engage the guards in conversation, but they were silent. Remembering that Murah in speaking to us had kept his distance, and after leaving the tent had gargled from a bowl of water, I felt a certain sense of security; while we were still "taboo" none of the Arabs would have the courage to touch us, much less prepare us for execution.

I explained to Allan that we were safe, at least for the moment. But if we were to prevent the sheik from sending us back to the tomb for the valuable objects, and give Aly enough time to get to Aswan, we must simulate a sickness that made it impossible for us to walk.

Twice a day food was brought to us and three times a day Murah came outside the tent to shout his questions about our current state of health. For three days we played our role as sick men, groaning at regular intervals. Late in the afternoon of the last day we heard commotion in the village. English voices!

"Thank heavens," I said. "Aly got off the telegram."

A few minutes later we were sitting with the Inspector of the Egyptian Department of Antiquities, Mustafa el-Gamel of Cairo, and the English captain who had come to our rescue with a platoon of men. Murah had hidden his chagrin and served us the customary peace offering of coffee.

When Allan and I, accompanied by the Inspector, entered the tomb again, the mummy was still sitting upright in his case. But another miracle had occurred. The gold *ankh* with chain and the necklace were missing. No Arab of the village would have dared to invade the tomb to steal them. The thief's identity remained a mystery.

The Inspector congratulated Allan upon his discovery of Reheme's tomb and made arrangements for the mummy and alabaster jars to be taken to Cairo's Egyptian Museum. It was. two years later that I discovered the *ankh* with its golden chain in the shop of a Cairo dealer in antiquities. The mystery of the stolen necklace had the same simple and human explanation. Aly, before escaping to Aswan, had gone into the tomb and taken both *ankh* and necklace. That was why Allan never heard from him again.

The Four Gold Coins

THE TIBERIAS heat was oppressive as I strolled to the shop of Mustafa, the goldsmith. The last time I had seen him was a year before, when I was vacationing in Tiberias and had found the ring of Julia Domna. My shirt was wet with perspiration as I entered Mustafa's shop, and I waited impatiently for him to offer me the customary cup of coffee. He had changed little. His long beard was white, but his strong dark eyes still had the same sparkle. I did not know much about Mustafa — only that he had four wives and a couple of dozen children and grandchildren. He was well to do; his shop had flourished for over forty years. Bartering with him for what valuable objects he might have would not be easy.

Our talk was personal. He wanted to know about my work, my family. I returned the compliment. Finally, after my third cup of coffee, when we had discussed his grandchildren and his pet, a profane parrot, I thought it time to come to the point.

My eyes searched the little shop. "No new finds?" I asked, couching my question in the negative.

"Nothing."

"I don't believe you, Mustafa, my old friend," I said. "Some of your *fellahin* must have brought you something."

He shook his head. His long-fingered, bony fingers caressed his beard. "By Allah, my friend, I have found nothing, and heard of nothing that has been found."

I saw a certain light in his eyes and was certain he was lying. Perhaps there was nothing in his shop to show me, but Mustafa had definitely heard of something that would be of interest to me.

I took some silver coins from my pocket and put them on his workbench.

"For your grandchildren — for sweets," I said.

Mustafa nodded thanks and sipped his coffee. He did not speak for ten minutes. Then he said, "My friend, have you ever been in Umm Qeis?"

"No," I said. "Why, has something been found there?"

"There is a rumor," Mustafa said casually.

I came alert. Certainly, I thought, something important has happened in Umm Qeis. "What do you know of it?" I asked with equal casualness.

"Nothing much. It is only village gossip. But a farmer of Umm Qeis is rumored to have found four gold coins. I do not know his name."

Umm Qeis was the ancient Gadara, where Julia Domna had spent her years of exile. Gadara had been destroyed by Moslem invaders in the seventh century A.D., and its amphitheater, temples, and marble statues of the gods and goddesses smashed to ruins. If Mustafa's information was correct, it was possible the four gold coins were from this period. Or perhaps they were from the time of Julia Domna herself.

On the other hand, I warned myself, the coins could be historically worthless. They were perhaps German, buried or lost during the World War I, when the Germans and Turks had fought in the Holy Land against the English. Or perhaps they were from the time of Napoleon, or only Turkish gold *piasters*, or Byzantine coinage. Seventeen hundred years had passed since Roman Gadara had flourished.

Was it really so essential for me to follow in bloodhound fashion the sparse information Mustafa had given me? I had come to Tiberias for a week's peace and relaxation, nothing more. Yet now, like a bad detective, I was on the trail of something that probably didn't exist. Why should I go to a remote village, into the rocky wilderness of the mountains of Gilead, in search of a Jordanian peasant whose name I did not even know?

The clues I had were nebulous, but the relentless archaeologist in me had accepted the challenge. I hastily packed my knapsack, and on my way to breakfast in the hotel, the words of my great teacher, Flinders Petrie, came to my mind: "Archaeologists are God's greatest optimists."

Shortly after seven I was in the market place, waiting for the Arab bus that would take me to Samakh, my first stop before Umm Qeis. In Samakh, the fishing and market town on the Sea of Galilee's north shore, I would have to change buses.

Samakh I have already described briefly in another chapter ("The Ring of Julia Domna"). When I arrived that morning it was the day of the weekly animal market, and the town was very much alive.

I went to see my friend, the *muktar* Achmed, who had often been helpful in vouching for me when Arabs of the surrounding villages had been reluctant to give me their trust. Achmed was the only man I knew who could give me information about the farmers of Umm Qeis, and the best way of reaching the village. If luck were with me, Achmed might even provide me with an introduction to the village elder.

When I told him what Mustafa had said, the *muktar* was dubious. He doubted that something of value had been found in Umm Qeis; if it had, he, the *muktar* of Samakh, would have known of it.

He warned me that the forty or fifty natives of Umm Qeis were proud, and suspicious of strangers. "My friend," he said, "do not go there. It is a strenuous trip and the villagers are hostile. Umm Qeis belongs to Transjordan, and remember, it does not fall under the British mandate's jurisdiction."

"Achmed," I smiled, "you should know me better than that. I don't scare easily; why should I fear the villagers at Umm Qeis?"

We sipped the coffee Achmed's fourteen-year-old son, Aly, had served, and the *muktar* persisted in trying to sway me from my course.

A glimmer of understanding came to me suddenly. Achmed wanted to be part of the deal. It seemed that four gold coins, imaginary or not, had a tremendous attraction, not only for me but for everyone to whom they were mentioned. When Achmed made his proposition, I saw I was right.

"Paul," he began, "Go back to your hotel in Tiberias. I will go to Umm Qeis and find this *fellah*. I will buy the coins, for I know the way to deal with the people of the mountains. Then I will come to Tiberias and give them to you."

I laughed aloud. "No, my good friend," I answered. "Should I have to buy the coins from you, I would have to be a millionaire. However," I said emphatically, "for any additional information you can give me I will pay your price. For example, what is the safest route to Umm Qeis?"

"That would be too complicated for your citified mind," he said, and clapping his hands, shouted for his son Aly. "My boy will accompany you. He knows the way and he knows the people, and for only small baksheesh I will lend him to you."

The boy could be very helpful; if he knew the people of the village, they would not regard me as a total stranger. I was also aware that should I track down the coins with Aly's help, Achmed's baksheesh would grow to respectable proportions.

Aly, a bright and handsome boy, and I left an hour later. The bus brought us to El-Hammi, two milleniums ago the site of a temple where Aphrodite was worshiped. Now El-Hammi was a health resort whose sulphur springs gushed healing waters. Rich Arabs from nearby towns came there to cure their ills. It was the last stop. From here on we had to walk.

I was pleased with Aly's company. He was both good-hearted and helpful, insisting upon shouldering my knapsack after we had lunched on goat's cheese and lemonade and were on our way toward the River Jarmuk.

In the cypress forests we did not feel the heat of the day and made good time, but once we were in the open fields we were obliged to slow down. The sun blazed, and the hot sun burned through the soles of my shoes. I pitied Aly with his bare feet. But the skin of his feet was so calloused that he did not feel the torturing heat. Gradually the fields gave way to wild formations of rock. Here and there grew plants, cacti and thistles. We were nearing the river.

When we reached the Jarmuk, I could see no bridge across the swollen waters.

"Aly," I said, "how are we to cross; there is no bridge. You led me the wrong way."

"No, *Chawadjah*," he assured me. "There is an old man with a boat. He will bring us to the other side."

I shielded my eyes with my hand in the blazing sun, but I could see no boat.

Aly had sat down near the river under a ledge of rock. "Where is your boatman?" I asked.

"We must wait. If Allah is good to us the boatman will come before the day is over."

I was furious. I wanted to go to Umm Qeis, and I had no intention of waiting for hours on the edge of the Jarmuk.

Aly smiled, showing his white teeth. "The day is still young. Rest, *Chawadjah*. It is cool here."

The boy's Oriental fatalism irritated me extremely. I looked at my watch and saw it was after two o'clock. Unless the boatman came soon it would be dark before we reached the village. I sat down next to Aly and saw he was already fast asleep.

I, too, must have fallen asleep, for suddenly I felt a hand on my shoulder. Opening my eyes, I saw a very old Arab bending over me.

"Are you the boatman?" I asked, happy he had come at last.

"I am the boatman."

We jumped to our feet. "Where is your boat?" I asked.

"Boat?" he said. "I never use it. But follow me and I will show you how to reach the other side."

Off went my shoes and socks. We followed the old man across the river, jumping from sand bar to rock and from rock to sandbar until we had reached the bank opposite. I was wet to the waist, but the sun dried me quickly. I rewarded our guide and he wished me luck, Allah's guidance, and the love of Mohammed.

Aly quickly found the narrow donkey path up the mountain, bordered by wild thistles and prickly cactus. He moved much faster than I. "Hasten, *Chawadjah*," he kept calling to me. "Make haste."

We climbed for more than two hours before we reached the rocky plateau above the village. Thirty feet below us stood the yellow-brown clay huts of Umm Qeis, resting peacefully under the setting sun. At the foothills of the mountain lay large stone blocks, remains of a Roman amphitheater, now overgrown by grass and weeds. The difficulties of climbing had made me forget my mission, but seeing these remnants of the amphitheater, my purpose was refreshed. The blocks served to remind me that the past was still alive.

Entering the village, we were immediately surrounded by a dozen Arab children, whose dark eyes looked at me with fear and curiosity. The village dozed in the late afternoon. The main street leading through it was dusty and dirty; the doors and windows closed.

I talked to the children, trying to make friends, but they were too shy to answer. Never before had they seen a European. The few women who came out of the houses were heavily veiled, for I was a man and a stranger. Like worried hens they gathered their children and shooed them away.

I regretted my hurried departure from Tiberias, for in my haste I had not changed from Western clothes to a *gallabiyya* and *kufia* (head-dress), my Arab garments. The atmosphere was strange, so strange that even little Aly looked at me as though he too found this man extraordinary.

In my best Arabic I asked one of the women to lead me to the village elder. My pronunciation must have been amusing, for she laughed, and I felt easier. I opened my knapsack and handed out to the children still surrounding me my secret ammunition: sweets and candies. Led by the chattering women and children, I found myself at the hut of the elder of Umm Qeis.

The elder, a proud Moslem, recited from the Koran all the phrases of welcome for an unbeliever. The courtyard was clean and I heard women's voices in the background as the coffee was served. Aly, who knew the elder, introduced me formally to the old Arab. He told him I was an old friend of his father, the *muktar;* that I had the honesty of a newborn camel and the riches of a man from the city.

The elder opened his toothless mouth in a wide grin. "Welcome to my house, O friend of Achmed the *muktar* of Samakh."

I crossed my arms and replied, "It will be an honor to be your friend."

As I told the elder the purpose of my visit to Umm Qeis, I saw doubt in his face.

Leaning forward earnestly, he pointed to his heart. "Believe me, if someone in my village had found gold coins I would know of it."

I listened carefully to what he went on to say, as the elder swore roundly that he knew nothing of the matter. Complimenting him on his authority and wisdom, I asked for the name of the peasant: not once had the elder mentioned the name of Mohammed or Allah in his oaths and protestations, and I knew he was lying.

I decided to gamble. I reached for my briefcase and casually opened my wallet so that he could see the pound notes within. I sipped my coffee, giving the old man time to make up his mind. By now he must have realized that I was a sharp trader too. After a long silence he began to tell me that he remembered vaguely that a long time ago one of the *fellahin* had found a clay jar. This was all he could remember.

I put my cup on the ground, and looked straight into his eyes. "Half a pound for the name of the peasant," I said.

"What is half a pound for the knowledge of a man's name? A man's name is sacred. You are a wealthy man, the friend of a *muktar.*" He launched into a recital of the misery of his life. "The crop last year was bad, the jackals laid waste to half my fields, the camels are too high in price and they are eating too much. My women are old now and I wait only for the pleasures of heaven, for by Allah," he sighed, "I have no money to buy a new wife."

I shook my head in commiseration, and doubled my offer.

"One pound," I said. The old man took up his lamentations again, his voice oily and pious. He stretched his arms toward Mecca.

"Why does Allah punish me so hard?" he wailed. "My information is surely worth two pounds to a decent man from Jerusalem. Oh Allah, do not shorten the years of my life!"

I couldn't help laughing. I wanted his information desperately, but my good name as a trader among the Arabs would have been compromised had I accepted his terms without a fight. And did he really know the name of the *fellah?* Did such a man exist, or was I wasting my hard-earned money?

"One pound or nothing," I said sharply.

My tone convinced the elder that this was my last offer, and he accepted it. The name of the *fellah* was Salim, he told me. At this time of day Salim was still at work in his field, and I would have to wait until nightfall to see him. This meant I had to spend the night in Umm Qeis, and I arranged for Aly and me to sleep in the elder's courtyard in my blankets and pup-tent. For the elder's hospitality I was obliged to give him another two shillings, but he addressed me now as *Achuya,* his brother.

Salim's clay hut, toward the middle of the village, was small and uncared-for. The village gossip had already reached his ears; I was greeted with sullen indifference. Two workworn women well over thirty-five, dressed in cheap blue serge, were busy over the hut's open fire. Half-filled sacks of grain leaned against the broken plastered walls. A few hungry chickens scratched for stray grains. Salim, a man of forty-five, sturdy, with a pock-marked face and shrewd eyes under a low forehead, was sharpening a scythe.

I stood and waited, but no one paid me the slightest attention. Finally

Salim threw down his scythe and said, "If you are looking for something people say I have found, I am not the man."

He turned back to his work. The man was afraid, but of what? Ignoring his statement, I said, "Mustafa in Tiberias would give you only the worth of your gold, but I would give you so much more that you could buy new clothes for both your wives."

Unimpressed, Salim did not answer. I was tired of standing and asked Salim's permission to sit on the ground. He nodded his head, his sharp eyes blinking at me. "Do as you wish, but I have nothing to sell to you."

From time to time the two women turned to look at me. Carefully I calculated my next step. You can trade or barter with an Arab only if he is willing to do the same, and Salim showed complete indifference. I repeated what I had said before, this time raising my voice when I mentioned the new clothes for his wives. Perhaps his women could persuade him. The result of my strategy was that Salim sent the women to their quarters.

After a while I lit a cigarette.

"*Ushrab*, Salim," I said, inviting him to smoke. To my surprise he responded. He accepted a cigarette and sat down beside me. At last he seemed willing to listen.

"Mustafa," I said, "would not have told me to make such a long trip unless for good reason."

"Mustafa is a liar," Salim said comfortably. "He knows nothing of what I have found."

"Ah, then you *have* found something."

In silence we puffed on our cigarettes.

"Are you really from Jerusalem and not from Amman?" he asked me. "Are you not sent by the Transjordan government?" It was true that the Transjordanian as well as other Middle Eastern governments sent out inspectors of antiquities who relieved farmers of their archaeological finds.

"By Allah, no!" I said emphatically. "I have nothing to do with your

Transjordan government. I am from Jerusalem. I am an archaeologist, a man who searches for relics of the past. I am not here to spy on you and take the coins away. I will buy them."

To substantiate my words I produced my credentials, but Salim was illiterate and could not read. So I showed him pictures of my wife and son posed before an Egyptian tomb, and for the first time his pock-marked face smiled. The game of barter had turned in my favor.

"I'll give you a good price if the coins are what I think they are," I said. "Show them to me."

"I will not sell them. I will only trade them."

"What would you like in exchange?"

Salim considered. "A camel four years old."

It would cost me eight Palestinian pounds for a camel. The price was worth it. I said: "It's a deal, Salim." Our handshake followed.

"Now, let me see the coins," I said.

He smiled. "Have I seen the camel?"

Reluctantly I agreed to the blind bargain. The details were arranged. In eight days I was to return to Salim's courtyard with the camel, and with many salaams we parted.

I returned to the elder's courtyard, where Aly waited for me. A good day's work had been done. During my lengthy conversation, Aly had been busy telling fantastic tales about me to the boys of the village. My reputation was made. The elder's eyes widened when I told him of the transaction; to him it was tremendous.

"A camel!" he cried. "A camel costs a great deal of money. You must be rich, *Chawadjah*." If he had only known how large a proportion of my monthly paycheck the camel represented, and how poorly my wife in Jerusalem would take my extravagance!

Reaching the Jarmuk on our way back the next morning, we did not wait for the guide, but remembering the way across, got to the other bank safely. In Samekh I gave the *muktar* baksheesh for Aly's help, and the boy some silver coins for himself. The animal market was closed, and I would have to wait another six days before it opened again.

In Jerusalem my friends were skeptical about the bargain with Salim. "You know how Arabs are," they said. "You can't trust them."

But I persisted in feeling that even the seductive atmosphere of Umm Qeis with its amphitheater ruins had failed to cloud my judgment. My methods might be unorthodox, but I would continue to invest in intuition. Only a few months before I had rejected an offer to join the Oriental Research Institute in Jerusalem. The offer was sound financially, but it would have prevented my doing research and excavation on my own. I refused to become a bookworm like most of my colleagues, researching so minutely and systematically that, before the first shovel sank into the earth of a ruin or a tomb, the prospective find was already known and classified. This was not my way. I felt that Salim's handshake was a firm link to the past, and I kept on believing in him.

Five days later I was in Samakh again, bartering for the best camel four-year-old I could find. I bought a proud and spirited animal whose name was Bala, who behaved as though she knew I was only her temporary master.

Aly and I made the trip to El-Hammi in under three hours. But when we came to the Jarmuk, Bala, afraid of the water, turned stubborn. Aly danced and clowned to please her, but Bala was not intrigued. Finally we had to beat the animal across to the opposite bank. As we went up the mountain Bala developed a tremendous hunger, stopping at every thistle and bush. Half way up she decided judiciously upon an extended nap.

I knew we had to hurry if we expected to reach Umm Qeis before nightfall. Aly's efforts to make Bala rise were crowned with failure. But then he had an idea, and began to pray into her hairy ear. The word "Allah" seemed to have a tremendous effect upon the camel. She rose with dignity, and from that point onward gave us no trouble.

Arriving in Umm Qeis, I went directly to Salim's house. I was proud; I had kept my promise. Today was the day we had agreed upon. Soon I would hold the four gold coins in my hand. But the Arab's reception was disconcerting. He mumbled the customary welcome and hardly glanced at Bala.

"I have brought your four-year-old," I said. "She is a good animal. Be good to her and she will serve you faithfully."

Salim grimaced wryly. I was angry; I had brought the price he had demanded and was unwelcome in his house.

"Salim," I said sternly, "let us close our deal."

He shrugged.

"A deal is a deal!" I shouted. "Take your camel and give me my coins!"

He shifted his feet; his eyes avoided mine as he said, *"Chawadjah,* there is something I must tell you. By Allah, it is not that I do not wish to keep my word. But only once in a lifetime does Allah send a poor *fellah* such a gift. I have prayed for guidance, but what is a camel against four such gold coins?"

So that was it. Salim had been corrupted, perhaps by the village elder. He wanted more money from me. So far my friends had been discouragingly right. I should never have started the whole business.

"Salim," I said, with a sinking heart, "you are a man of faith. You believe in Allah and in Mohammed, and you cannot break your word. It was not a simple matter for me to buy the camel and bring it to Umm Qeis. I have kept my part of the bargain and will accept no excuses from you."

"Chawadjah," Salim began his litany, "only once in a lifetime does a man — " but I interrupted him. "You are wrong," I said. "There are many moments in a man's lifetime. Perhaps tomorrow, perhaps a year from now, Allah will send you another jar with gold coins."

"That is impossible. I have dug in my fields everywhere, but there is no other jar."

I was determined not to give in. Furious, I demanded the gold coins. Salim must have sensed my firmness of purpose, for he came quickly to the point.

"Please, *Chawadjah,* do not shout so. It is not that I dislike the camel. But I do not really need her. I would like to exchange her for a good cow and three mother sheep. Then, by Allah, I swear I will give you the coins."

"You should have thought of this before. I contracted to bring you a camel."

We entered into a competition of silence. For half an hour we stared at the ground, saying nothing. Finally Salim said, "Come, I will show you something."

He led me outside to the courtyard and to his small stable. Opening the wooden door, he showed me a well-fed donkey.

"With my two wives, he is strong enough to plow the land. Therefore you see, *Chawadjah,* I need no camel."

Should I leave, and renounce the coins, taking Bala with me? Salim was watching me carefully. Finally I said, "If I exchange the camel for a cow and sheep then you must show me the coins. I will not make another blind bargain with you."

His forehead wrinkled in thought.

"No," he said, "that I cannot do."

"Then we have no bargain!" I shouted. Undoubtedly the coins were worthless. Still — and I ground my teeth at my uncertainty — I couldn't be entirely sure; Salim himself had no accurate way of assessing the coins' value. I said: "Then at least let me see the jar in which you found them."

He looked at me, puzzled, but without argument went inside his house and brought out a small clay jar, about three and a half inches high. The jar was in excellent condition, and I saw with excitement that its string design was typical of the late Roman periods of Antoninus Pius, Septimus Severus, and Julia Domna. When I moistened the jar with a little water it dried instantly, proof it was genuine and no copy by an Umm Qeis potter. My doubts were gone. The coins Salim had found inside the jar must be Roman.

Seeing I was pleased with the jar he said, with the gesture of a nobleman, "It is yours — take it."

We sealed our second bargain.

In Samakh the next morning the animal market had not yet opened, but I found Bala's former owner sitting in a side-street coffeehouse.

"Your camel," I said, "is a good one, but I must exchange it for a cow and three female sheep."

The Arab looked at me shrewdly. "I cannot take the camel back. It is sold. But I have a very good cow and also sheep that I could sell to you."

Aly and I tried to sell Bala elsewhere. But we found no customers in Samakh. Poor Bala had become absolutely worthless on her journey to and from Umm Qeis. I bought fodder and paid for a stall in the stable, and the next morning was forced to sell the camel for less than a quarter of what I had paid for her. Aly negotiated with a dealer for a cow and sheep, and we started back to the village.

The cow swam tractably enough across the Jarmuk, but we had to carry the sheep in our arms. Climbing the mountain, the trip this time was less onerous. I knew Salim would keep his bargain, and I would see my coins at last.

When our procession entered the village the children of Umm Qeis surrounded us, shouting and laughing, and I took this as a good omen. Salim did not await us in his courtyard but ran toward me, waving his arms and crying aloud. He examined the animals and, well satisfied, embraced me. Then he ran back into the house, and when he returned I saw gold glitter in the palm of his hand.

I could hardly repress my eagerness to see the coins, but Salim kept his fist closed upon them.

"You are my brother," he said. "You are a good man and can help me."

I sighed. What did the man want of me now?

"Have you seen my two wives?" he asked. I nodded. "They are no good," he muttered. Oh no, I wondered fearfully; he could not want to sell them to me.

"I am still a young man, yet I have no son. My two women are useless for breeding. You are an understanding man. With your help I could be the father of a son."

I looked at him, bewildered.

"There is a village not far from here," he said. "Ibrahim lives there with a healthy fourteen-year-old daughter. She could be the mother of my son. *Achuya*, Ibrahim asks only eight pounds for the girl. I have six. Lend me two pounds."

I laughed. So that was what he wanted.

I smiled. "Let me see the coins first."

He opened his fist slowly, and one by one gave me the coins.

They were four perfect Roman gold coins in practically mint condition. On the face of the first was stamped the head of Antonius Pius; on the second, that of his son, Septimus Severus; on the third, that of his wife, Julia Domna, who had been in exile in Umm Qeis when it was still Gadara, and whose sealstone ring I had found at the bottom of the Sea of Galilee.

I examined the fourth coin and could hardly believe my eyes. It was that of the Emperor Caracalla, her son. The reverse side bore four figurines that represented the four seasons. I knew that Caracalla in A.D. 214 had instructed his mint-master to design the *felicia tempora*, which he gave as medals to his most trusted friends. Only one *felicia tempora* had ever been found, and it was now in the private collection of Britain's ruling family.

I clapped Salim on the shoulder. "You are still a strong man," I said, "and must become the father of a son."

I thought Salim's two wives would be disturbed to hear of his impending marriage, but on the contrary they shared their husband's joy. A fire was lit in the courtyard and we had our meal together. The elder who had led me to Salim joined us. I promised to send him a gift from Jerusalem.

Salim and I left the next morning for Faralla, the village of Ibrahim, and I served as witness for the Moslem marriage contract. I gave Salim three pounds more for the promise that if he became the father of a son I would be the child's godfather. The marriage was set for the following week, but business in Jerusalem prevented my attending.

Four gold coins and reverse, each 1″ in diameter.

Among my colleagues the discovery of the Roman coins, worth a current $4,000, created a sensation. I got weary of telling the story of Salim and Umm Qeis.

A year later I received a letter from Mustafa, the goldsmith of Tiberias. He told me that Salim was the father of a son. He had named the boy Dahab Ibn Salim, which means "Gold, the son of Salim."

» XI «

The Story of Ragah

OUTSIDE Jerusalem, between Gethsemane and the Mount of Olives, lies the Valley of Hinnom, Ge-Hinnom. For me Ge-Hinnom had more of the atmosphere of ancient times than most other places in Jerusalem. It was a lovely spot and, escaping from my work and studies in the city, I would take long walks in the narrow valley filled with cyprus and oleanders. Centuries-old tombstones dotted the ground; the monument to Absalom and the granite and marble family burial places, dating back to the time of the Maccabees and the Roman occupation of Jerusalem, were my special interest.

The Valley itself had now no particular archaeological significance, for heavy excavation work had already been carried out and every tombstone, necropolis, and ruin was known, researched, and written about. But the Valley's historical importance was considerable. During the course of history many invading armies had encamped here while besieging Jerusalem, among them the Babylonians of Nebuchadnezzar and the Romans of Vespasian and Titus. Here the Maccabeans had secretly stored their weapons, and the Hebrew Zealots trained for guerrilla warfare against the Roman oppressors.

At the Valley's end were the ruins of the huts where the lepers had lived, well isolated from the pulsating life of the city. Not far from the leper's huts were the tombs of those slaughtered by the Roman child king, Elagabalus. The Valley was full of reminders of the follies and glories of the past.

Here I could dream and relive history. In a way I thought of it as my secret place, and certainly I had never considered it in professional terms.

During the days following my discovery of the glassware at Cana, I sought seclusion in Ge-Hinnom for still another reason. The Cana finds had involved me in a disturbing controversy. It had been impossible for me to prevent any of the widespread religious "deductions" that had followed the Cana expedition. Yet, while I had never myself linked the Cana finds with any specific religious event, for me they were more than archaeological objects. They had the lure of the Bible. They were from the time of Christ, found in a two-thousand-year-old house in a village described in the Gospels as a place where a miracle had been performed. Was it not possible they were some kind of revelation from the past? Had I not gone to Cana on the kind of hunch that rarely failed me? Though I had found no rational answers to these questions I believed that answers existed, and no amount of skeptical scoffing could persuade me differently. The only concession I made to the doubters was to keep my silence as they aired their disbelief.

In the first few weeks after returning from Cana I was at the Valley often. Villages for miles around sent their sheep to graze there, and almost daily I would see the flocks, each in the care of an aged shepherd. These old men received small pay for their work and a percentage of the lambs born yearly. It was an ancient profession, one passed down from father to son.

I came to know these shepherds, and often we sat together and talked. The best grassland was in the southern outskirts of the Valley not far from the Gardens of Gethsemane and, sitting there with my friends, I could see to the left the skyline of Jerusalem, dominated by the shining cupola of the Mosque of Omar on Mount Moriah. To the right were the slopes of the Mount of Olives, now cultivated in terraces for the growing of wine grapes, but once proud with the palaces and villas of the high priests, keepers of the temple, Roman patricians, and noble Hebrews. Mary Magdalene's villa had once stood there, and the summer house of Pontius Pilate.

The old shepherds knew a great deal about the Valley, and told me stories never written and events never recorded. Pious Moslems devoted to the Koran and the teachings of Mohammed, the Valley was their entire world. As long as the grass grew each spring, as long as their sheep were healthy and their lambs born in sufficient number, they had no worries. Their attitudes, their way of thinking and talking, reflected what their life's work had taught them, and it seemed that between these shepherds and their flocks existed a kind of intuitive understanding. Both belonged to the landscape; missing either, an essential part of it would have been lost.

One day in the Valley, walking on the southern slope of the Mount of Olives, my eye fell idly upon a walled rock formation descending from the Mount directly into the Valley. This formation, about three hundred yards long, was known for its cave tombs that had already been excavated. During the reign of Herod Antipas and the Roman governorship of Judea, the caves had been the burial place for those who had revolted against and been crucified by the Judean Roman authorities. But not only these rebels were buried here; the caves had been used as a local cemetery for the last few hundred years, sealed simply by rolling a heavy rock or stone before the opening.

Approaching closer to the rock formation, I noticed a stone, half hidden by shrubbery, which I thought might be the entrance to a cave. Pushing aside the shrubbery, I carefully examined the stone, which appeared to be part of the natural rock. I went over the stone inch by inch with my magnifying glass, and found, at one side, earth with grass growing sparsely from it. I scratched the earth away with my pocket-knife and the blade, suddenly meeting no resistance, plunged in to the hilt. I was puzzled. I looked for a long twig to insert in the opening, but those I found were too thick. Then I had an idea. I took a page from my notebook, folded it carefully, and inserted it into the crack. It penetrated to its entire length, about five inches, without interference.

I was convinced now that the stone, about two feet wide and three feet high, was not part of the natural rock but had been rolled here by human hands. During a period of almost two thousand years it had undoubtedly become cemented to the rock formation.

Twilight had fallen in the valley. I took out my flashlight and trained its beam over the stone's surface, searching for an ancient tomb inscription. Very often on such stones the names of the buried were chiseled either in Aramaic or Hebrew lettering. There were many indentations, and one — not more than two inches in diameter — I thought might be man-made. But the light was too bad for me to come to any definite conclusion. I took another sheet from my notebook, wet it with my tongue and pressed it against the indentations, waiting until the paper clearly bore their impress. Without question, the lines were the formation of the ancient Hebrew letter *Resh*, comparable to the Latin letter *R*. Feeling further with my fingertips, I thought I detected other illegible letters worn away by time.

I scraped away with my pocketknife into the opening, but centuries of dust had locked the rock into the hillside, and my efforts to dislodge it were futile. Then I had another idea. I wrote my name and the date on another piece of paper, folded it, and inserted it into the opening. My ear to the slit, I listened to determine how long it took the paper to fall. Perhaps a second had passed before I heard the paper strike the ground. Now I was certain I had discovered a tomb, and like a dog I sniffed at the opening to see if I could detect a tomb's peculiar mold and cinnamon odor.

But without the proper tools I could do nothing, and before excavating further I was obliged to report the tomb to the Department of Antiquities; the entire valley was, so far as archaeological research was concerned, under their jurisdiction. Perhaps I would be able to return the next day with helpers and the proper authorization to excavate.

Next morning at the Monastery of St. Anne I told Father Fleurant of my discovery. Together we went to the Rockefeller Museum to Dr. R. W. Hamilton. Hamilton, though an old friend, was an inveterate skeptic when it came to my enthusiastic discoveries.

"It's quite impossible that you have found a tomb here," he told me. "Everything in the area has been registered and catalogued for more than sixty years. I doubt very much that you have found something missed by every other archaeologist before you."

"But Rick," I protested, "there's absolutely no doubt. I ask only for your permission to remove the stone blocking the cave entrance."

Hamilton regarded me with quizzical amusement. "Well, since I can't believe there's anything there, logically I can hardly withhold permission to you to look for it. Granted."

The next morning I returned to Ge-Hinnom with two of my Domitio seminar students and three personal friends, among them Father Fleurant. Under my direction we began the long and wearing work of removing the stone before the cave. Gripping it firmly, all six of us pulled with all our might, but the stone refused to budge. We drove spikes into it, tied rope around them, and pulled again. Still no success. We shoveled to remove dirt and earth from around the stone, and I asked my students to drive crowbars into the mountainside along the stone's edge.

We pulled and tugged, slipping, groaning and puffing. We were about to stop for a rest when the stone began to move. As we worked with renewed strength the stone for the first time in centuries slipped slowly from its niche.

There was now a gaping hole in the mountainside where the stone had lain. I paused triumphantly, but then we heard a pattering sound, like that of rain, and in a matter of seconds the mountain gravel had avalanched and filled in the hole completely.

"The shovels!" I shouted.

Like madmen we flew at the fresh dirt. Each shovelful we removed was replaced by new dirt sliding from the roof of the cavity. But angry and sweating and furious, I refused to give in.

I realized the hole would have to be braced as we dug it. We did so with thick branches from the nearby trees, and at last the roof began to hold. Two hours later we had enlarged the opening until it was big enough for a man to crawl through. The others stepped aside; now was my moment of discovery.

Dropping to my knees, I looked inside the cave. My body blocked the fading sunlight, and the interior was too dark for me to see anything within. I searched for my flashlight, conscious of the risk of snakes and scorpions. I had crawled halfway inside the cave when my hand touched the scattered bones of a skeleton. I immediately moved to one side and switched on my flashlight. Now I could see the cave was low but fairly long. I knocked my head against the shallow ceiling, and loose dirt poured down my neck in a steady stream.

I crawled closer to the skeleton. Centuries of ants had eaten the bones dry, and as I touched them the remnants of garment crumbled to dust. My flashlight revealed a scrap of withered cork, the remains of sandals, typical footwear of the people of Jerusalem during the Roman occupation. The sandals told me the tomb was at least nineteen hundred years old. But there were no tear glasses, no pottery vessels, no necklaces.

The dim light did not allow me to determine whether the skeleton was that of a male or that of the more delicately boned female. I asked my friends to bind rope around my feet so that I might be pulled out quickly if the cave ceiling collapsed, and went deeper into the cavern.

A few feet farther in I found the skull. It was when I was playing my flashlight over the dirt and sand of the area in which the skull had lain that I found them: two large gold earrings two inches long and in the shape of elongated ovals. They were of magnificent composition and design, and I quickly identified them as Roman-Etruscan, of the first century A.D.

When I left the cave the earrings were hidden deep in my pocket. In the blinding sunlight I saw that a number of natives had gathered to watch our work. It was time now to close the tomb. To replace the stone was too big an undertaking, and I thought it wise immediately to inform the Department of Antiquities, and ask them to send workmen to do the

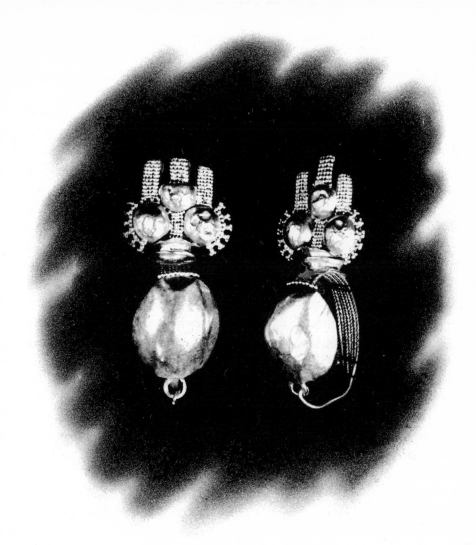

Gold earrings of Ragah, 2⅜" long.

job. Father Fleurant went to the nearest telephone while I rested in the shade.

A few minutes later the Father dropped to my side. He smiled at me. "Tell me, did you really find nothing in the tomb?"

I could hold back my secret no longer. I whispered to him, "I found a pair of gold earrings so magnificent that I have never seen their like before!"

When the Department workers arrived we returned to the city. I called Hamilton and promised him a full report. He was pleased about the earrings. I knew I would have a hard time keeping them, but with Hamilton on my side I stood a good chance.

I studied my find before my friends arrived that evening. The earrings' oval shape represented women's breasts and symbolized fertility; the cluster of grapes at their flanges represented riches and nobility. They could have been worn only by a Roman or Hebrew noblewoman of the first century. Why, then, had their owner been buried in a cave in the Valley of Ge-Hinnom, reserved for the political and criminal outcasts of Roman society?

Lovingly mounted by my wife on a piece of black velvet, the earrings looked extraordinarily beautiful. The last of their admirers to arrive was Father Fleurant, his white beard neatly combed. Commenting on the earrings he said, "The brutal time of Pontius Pilate comes alive in them," and we all nodded in silent agreement. Though we debated for some time the identity of their original owner, none of us came up with a solution.

In the next few days I received permission from Hamilton to keep the earrings. The tomb and skeleton, which was identified as female, became the property of the Department of Antiquities. The stone that had sealed the cave entrance was transported to the cellar of the Museum and its faded identations were definitely identified as a word beginning with the letter *R*.

Weeks passed. I was busy with research work for a European university. One evening, over a month later, Father Fleurant came to see me, carrying a bulky volume under his arm. Its parchment pages in Latin script were yellow with age. A chronicle from the year 1427, he had found it in his library among the old folios. The book had been written at the same time as the *Gesta Romanorum,* the famous Latin storybook. In it Fleurant had found a legend told to the ancient writer by Christian pilgrims who had visited the Christian shrines of the Holy Land in the time of Christ.

"Wasn't the letter on the ancient stone a *Resh?*" he asked me.

I nodded.

He smiled. "Then let me read to you the story of Ragah."

And here is the legend from the old chronicle substantially as Father Fleurant read it to me, retold in modern narrative style, based on the notes I made from the original book.

Poverty, misery, and hate overshadowed the land. From Jerusalem to Beer-sheba and from Sidon to Damascus, the people were held in slavery. Their children had been carried away to be servants of the conquerors, or to die young from the labors of unloading the ships from the West, or building the vast viaducts. Rome was without mercy, its leaders pitiless. Roman legionnaires with their short swords were everywhere at a word, ready to kill. Rome needed money for these troops, and to provide it the people of Judea, Galilee, and Sidon were bled white with taxes. Oppression bred hate, and hatred divided the people. No one knew who was friend or foe.

And there was one man who was feared and hated above all others. Pontius Pilate, Procurator of Judea.

There was unrest in Jerusalem, in Bethsaida, in the villages of the mountains, in the cities, the plains, in Galilee, and in the coastal towns. Secret groups had formed in all these, but they were poorly organized and divided by religion and tradition, for not only the Hebrews of Judea were under the heel of Rome, but also the people of Sidon and other cities where the Greek gods were still worshiped.

With Roman ears everywhere, the people were afraid to talk openly of their hatred. Spies lurked in the temple in Jerusalem and in the temples of the Greek gods, and when the people prayed they did so in whispers. Though the underground movement grew from day to day, it had few weapons. Nor could the hungry fight Rome's well-fed legionnaires. Only one weapon could be used with any effectiveness — assassination. And Pilate was the man marked for it above all others.

The handful of leaders of the Sidonian underground met each month in the Temple of Aphrodite to work out their plans for his murder. Each month the plans were changed. Pilate, his palace at Caesarea surrounded by an army of guards, was well protected. Any attempt to penetrate the palace guard would have been suicide. Though the Sidonians were prepared to die for their freedom, they knew that reckless daring was for fools.

One day a spy, returning from Jerusalem, reported that Pilate would go to Jerusalem for the high holidays of the Hebrews without taking his full guard with him.

The leader of the underground knew this was an opportunity he could not lose. There were many volunteers among the conspirators for a deed they felt would ignite a world-wide revolt against the Romans, but Vema, high priestess of the temple of Aphrodite, said the task was one for a woman.

The men regarded her doubtfully.

"Many festivities will be held at the palace during Pilate's stay in Jerusalem," said the high priestess. "Pilate is a man with a lust for life. He wants dancing and feasting. Though his guests will be screened carefully, the entertainers should be free to come and go without hindrance. There are forty dancing priestesses in the temple. They are all lovely; their art should enchant any man. Any one of them would be honored to kill Pilate."

Excitement swelled through the room. Should the Sidonians send entertainers to Pilate's festivities, such a gesture would be considered a friendly act. Perhaps the strict Roman surveillance in Sidon would be relaxed enough after the assassination so that sabotage might begin.

The project's good and bad points were discussed and rediscussed by the men. If the priestess who was chosen danced like a goddess before Pilate's guests, then surely Pilate would want her to entertain him privately in his chambers. A few moments alone with him would be enough for the assassin to plunge her dagger into his heart.

"It is almost time for the priestesses to dance their evening worship to Aphrodite," said Vema. "Watch with me from the high altar."

Inside the temple eunuchs lit the torches which hung on the marble columns. On the altar oil lamps glowed. Young postulants standing in the shadows held aloft bowls of burning incense. Sprigs of myrtle were placed on the altar steps, and the rose petals and golden apples sacred to Aphrodite.

A gong sounded. Silk curtains opened on the sides of the vast temple chamber and the young priestesses entered. Each maiden carried a white rose which she placed on the shining sanctuary floor; then, in the same formation, the forty priestesses returned to the center of the temple, and with heads bowed, faced the altar, waiting.

The soft music of the lutes began, and the dancers swayed gracefully. When the tinkling sound of systrums was heard, the dancers raised their arms in supplication, and on the first crash of the cymbals, began their dance. Outside in the square the people, knowing the service had commenced, lifted their voices in murmured prayers.

Behind the high altar the conspirators watched the dancing priestesses. The dancers were dressed alike in delicate veils thin as summer clouds. On their wrists and ankles were silver bracelets, and in their hair tiaras of myrtle leaves and flowers. The music became faster, the dancing more passionate and abandoned. Behind the altar the conspirators studied the dancers. All were beautiful; it would be hard to choose among them.

Suddenly Vema stiffened, and pointed to the rear of the temple. Five Roman soldiers who had dared to violate the privacy of the worship stood at the open door. The dancers stopped. But then one among them stepped forward, and going to the nearest marble column, reached up and grasped a flaming torch. She hurled it at the soldiers, and fiery sparks flew at their feet.

"Burn!" the priestess cried. "May all of you burn to death and ashes!"

The expression of astonishment on the Romans' faces changed to one of amusement, and shaking their heads, they turned away. The music began again and the priestesses resumed their dancing. Only the dancer who had thrown the torch stood aside, weeping. Small and lissome, she was younger than the others. Her skin was like ivory, her black hair like silk, her legs graceful as a gazelle's.

Vema remarked that the Romans had killed this girl's parents and brother.

"What is her name?" the leader asked.

"Ragah," the high priestess replied.

The brutal Procurator was awaited as the feast of Passover began. The spirits of the thousands of worshipers were dampened, and when it became known that Sidon had sent an entertainer for Pilate the people of Jerusalem wept, for they thought the Sidonians had weakened in their hatred and resolve. Had their neighbors to the North, whom the Hebrews had considered their allies, suddenly turned traitor like the Pharisees and many of the rich? As Ragah's caravan approached the center of the city the people thronged the streets for a look at her. The crowds murmured their disapproval, and among the young men of the Judean underground there were hotheads who would have thrown her from her litter and disfigured her as a punishment.

Riding heavily veiled through the narrow streets, Ragah heard the harsh words and imprecations. She drew back her veil to let the people see her face. The angry murmurs faded into whispered surprise at her beauty. Proudly Ragah played her role.

Among the many young men in the streets was one who could not take his eyes from the visitor. He was wealthy and reputed to be dissolute;

only a few knew that he, Nahum, nephew of Caiaphas, the collaborating high priest, was a leader of the Hebrew underground.

Turning to his friend Aran, Nahum whispered, "She is beautiful. How can such loveliness be wasted on such swine?"

Aran smiled bitterly. "She is not for you, Nahum, but for Pilate. All good things are reserved for the Romans."

Ragah's caravan moved through Jerusalem to a small house and garden on the outskirts of the city. Here she would stay until she danced for Pilate. Amyu, the eunuch, and an emissary from Sidon went to the palace high on Mount Moriah to talk to Pilate's master of ceremonies. The arrangements were quickly made. Ragah was to dance on the concluding night of the festivities, when Pilate would entertain the Roman nobles and wealthy Pharisees.

When the emissary returned he urged that she rest, saying she would need all her beauty and courage for the feast. "And remember," he said, "to conquer a Roman heart needs time and a wooden face. Be patient."

With high hopes the emissary returned to Sidon, leaving Ragah under the authority and protection of the eunuch Amyu.

The festival began, and soon there were only two days before its conclusion. Ragah used the time well. Skins filled with goat's and camel's milk stood ready for her bath, and exotic spices were brought from the market place. Cinnamon and myrrh, amber and henna, and fragrant perfumes of Egypt, Babylon, and Smyrna were used to anoint and salve her. That night she prayer for hours before the marble statue of Aphrodite the Nubian guards had carried all the way from her city.

On the concluding night of the festival the vast banquet hall echoed from the talk and laughter of the many guests who sprawled on pillows at the low tables. On a dais at the far end of the hall was Pilate's table. With him sat the first Roman centurion of Judea, Claudia, Pilate's wife, and Domena, his favorite mistress. Opposite the dais, at the other end of the hall, were the Hebrew leaders of Judea and Galilee, rich sheiks from the desert, and the nobility of Cyprus and Alexandria, among them Caiaphus, high priest of the temple, in his place of honor. Behind Caiaphus sat his nephew Nahum. Slaves brought heaping platters of food and constantly refilled the wine cups. The guests' mutual resentment vanished as the wine flowed and the merriment increased.

In the middle of the hall, reserved for the performers, dwarfs tumbled and wrestlers showed their skill; the winners were rewarded with pieces of gold and silver. For more than two hours the feast continued; then suddenly there was a beating of drums, and the guests fell silent. Louder and louder sounded the drum beats, as four huge Nubian slaves appeared carrying a large basket, which they lowered before Pilate's dais. A ram's horn blew, and the lid was removed. As the drums and lute and other instruments joined one another two hands rose exquisitely from the basket.

Then Ragah stood, and stepped from the basket. She held her arms high above her and her body swayed. Clad only in a veiled tunic, the whiteness of her body shone through it. The drumbeat grew louder and the dance began. Ragah whirled and twisted, her arms held out as if in entreaty to Pilate. She swayed to the music as though the floor were not marble but the flower-strewn glade of a forest temple. Then, as the tempo increased, the dance became frantic in its provoking sensuality. The male guests leaned forward, breathing heavily. On the dais, Pilate's eyes followed the dancer's every movement. Again there came the wailing of the ram's horn, and the dance was ended. Ragah stood before the dais motionless.

Never before had Jerusalem seen such dancing. The guests shouted and cheered as the dancer stepped forward and knelt before Pilate. With a gesture of his hand Pilate silenced them.

His eyes were fixed in admiration and desire upon the girl. "Dancer from Sidon, you are beautiful, and know how to use your body. I will reward you as no other Roman can."

He clapped his hands. A servant approached with a wooden jewel box. The Procurator took up a handful of jewels and let them fall through his fingers.

"None of these jewels is beautiful enough," he said, and looked toward his wife Claudia, who wore gold earrings in the form of cupids. Pilate's eyes wandered further till they rested upon his mistress Domena. She also wore heavy gold earrings, shaped like clusters of grapes.

He pointed toward his mistress, and ordered that Domena's earrings be taken off and soldered upon the ears of Ragah. As the smith approached her Domena screamed, and he needed the help of two heavily muscled Nubians to remove them from her.

When the earrings had been soldered Ragah stood erect, and a sigh of admiration escaped the crowd. Again Ragah, more beautiful than before, bowed before the Procurator, triumph in her eyes.

Her dance had excited Pilate. This woman, this flower of Asia, promised all the exotic pleasures of the East, and he was anxious for her to share his bed. He told her the earrings were a passport to his quarters, and that when she wore them no guard would stop her. He gave her permission to retire, and in silence she left the hall. In the courtyard Amyu greeted her with excited congratulations, but there was a feeling of heaviness in her she could not explain, and she responded with a wan smile. A dark cloud overshadowed her heart. As a woman she should have been pleased that the most important Roman in Judea had found her desirable and given her a priceless gift. But she felt that the decisive part of her mission was not as easily to be fulfilled.

Amyu touched the golden earrings. "These," he said smilingly, "are the keys to Pilate's death chamber."

Troubled, Nahum asked himself if he loved this woman his friends believed was a cheap courtesan, willing to share the Roman conqueror's bed. But in his heart he knew she was no courtesan; the triumph he had seen in her eyes as she accepted the earrings had been more than the vaingloriousness of a superficial woman. Instinctively he felt her purpose might be other than it seemed.

In the palace courtyard he had watched her enter the curtained litter and seen the four Nubians carry it off. Amyu, mounted on a donkey, had trailed after. Nahum had followed through the winding streets to the small house on the outskirts of the city. Hiding nearby, he had seen Ragah enter the house. Then he had boldly knocked on the door, but the Nubians had refused him entrance, telling him insultingly that only Romans were allowed in this house.

He had gone away, furious.

Later that night he met with the other leaders of the underground. There was much talk about the feast and gossip about Ragah, Pilate's gift, and Domena's humiliation.

Their leader Simon, most fanatical of the young Hebrews, talked of their next raid against the Romans. While Pilate was in Jerusalem, the Procurator should witness the strength of the underground, which in two days' time would attack the Roman stables near the fortress of Antonia.

Ragah had a restless night, plagued by a premonition of disaster. The next morning she listlessly drank her sweetened milk, lonely for the temple in Sidon. When Amyu entered the garden frowningly she knew something was amiss. He asked if she had friends or acquaintances in Jerusalem, and Ragah replied that this was the first time she had been here.

"Last night," said Amyu, "a man followed you home from the palace. When he asked entrance to the house, the servants barred his way."

Ragah looked at him wonderingly. What reason would this man have to see her? Amyu told her that the Pharisees, friendly to the Romans, might well suspect their purpose here. They must be watchful. He would try to find out something about this young man. Meanwhile, Ragah was not to leave the house without him.

When the stars were out over the eternal city, she sat in the garden watching the narrow street. It was quiet and deserted. Almost an hour had passed before she realized that someone was standing in the shadow of a nearby olive tree.

He was young, handsome, beardless. She followed his gaze as his eyes searched her house, passing over the dark corner where she sat. She heard him sigh, then watched him move away. She was curious about him, but she dared not speak.

Amyu awoke her at midnight. The identity of the spy, he told her, had been established. He was Nahum, son of Caiaphus, the Hebrew high priest, and a member of the rebel band led by Simon. It was Simon and his men who last month had burned the Roman warehouse.

Undoubtedly Simon suspected them and had assigned Nahum to watch the house.

Ragah looked doubtful.

"What other reason can there be?" said Amyu. "Unless," and he smiled, "Nahum saw your dance and has conceived a passion for you."

Ragah lay awake in the darkness, glad she had not told Amyu she had seen the young Hebrew. She could not believe he was really a spy, for he had shown no stealth or caution. Perhaps Amyu was right, and this handsome young man admired — even loved — her. What was love, she wondered. She had never felt love, though she had read of it in the books of Euripides and Socrates and other Greek writers. In the temple where she served and in her life there was room for only two kinds of love: love for her goddess Aphrodite and for her people. What must the other kind of love be like?

Going to the window, she looked out upon the darkness of the street, wishing she could see again the young Hebrew's face. And she felt her loneliness and the duty of her mission heavily upon her. Why, out of all the temple priestesses, had she been chosen to kill Pilate? For the first time, thinking of the handsome young Hebrew, she resented the self-sacrifice her mission entailed.

Awakening late the next morning she examined the earrings. They were beautiful, but they were evil too. They meant Pilate expected her to give herself to him when she received his invitation to dance privately before him, and that she would never do. She would wait for him only to embrace her, and then she would plunge the dagger into his back, fast and deep, before he could cry for help.

Early the following morning a messenger from the palace arrived with Pilate's summons. The Procurator demanded to see the dancer before him at ten o'clock that night.

All day Amyu supervised Ragah's preparations. He was at her side as she bathed in the goat's milk. He stood near as the maids salved and perfumed her body. It was he who chose the cloudlike silken gown she would wear and her jewelry, making sure that none of her gems would outshine Pilate's earrings.

Amyu told her that after the deed was done he would wait for her here, in the garden. They would leave for Sidon immediately, and when the guards found Pilate's body in the morning, they would be safely on their way.

As Ragah entered her litter, she glanced toward the trees to see if Nahum were there, but the garden was empty. As the Nubians set off for the palace she was calm, determined not to fail her countrymen's trust. She thought of her family, dead at the hands of the Romans, and felt a renewed desire for revenge.

In a few hours she would quit Jerusalem forever. Yet the thought had its bitterness too, for it meant she would never again see the handsome young Hebrew.

When the litter reached the palace gates she heard the guards' harsh voices commanding the Nubians to halt. She parted the curtains and looked out. A quarter-mile away the sky was red and yellow with towering flames.

"Those damn rebels have fired the stables," said the guard. Approaching closer he noticed the earrings.

"Pontius Pilate waits for me," she said.

Grinning, the guard observed that the Procurator this night would have little time for entertainment.

In the courtyard couriers scurried in and out. A personal servant of Pilate's, seeing the earrings, quickly escorted her through the corridors to Pilate's chambers. The doorway was choked with legionnaires and centurions. When she entered the room Pilate looked up in surprise.

"I am very busy," he told her stiffly. "Urgent matters of state command my attention.

Ragah bowed, and asked if he preferred that she return some other night.

Pilate considered; then, "No," he said, "I will show these brigands Rome is still their master, and then you shall dance for me."

A high-ranking Roman officer pushed into the room, and bowing deep before Pilate, said that Simon, leader of the Hebrew underground, had been taken.

Pilate ordered that Simon at once be questioned for the names of his men. The officer told Pilate Simon had already refused to speak, and the Procurator shouted that the rebel leader be brought to him.

Ragah's heart beat violently. Amyu had said Nahum was one of Simon's men, and suddenly she feared he had been captured with him.

As Simon was thrust into the room, Pilate motioned to Ragah to take a seat in the rear of the chamber. The rebel's face was streaked with blood. When Pilate ordered him to speak Simon was silent. Pilate took a whip from one of the guards, and lashed it over Simon's face.

"So be it," Pilate said. "If you will not speak to me now, then your tongue will not be needed to speak to lesser men." He turned to his legionnaires. "Cut his tongue out!"

Perhaps two minutes later Ragah heard a sudden anguished scream. Then there was silence.

Pilate said that his mood had changed. He would send for her on some other more pleasant occasion.

Back in the garden Amyu was waiting for her. He was bitter that Simon had chosen this night to fire the stables.

Jerusalem was quiet the next morning. The shops were closed, the streets empty. The temple overflowed with Hebrews mourning Simon's death.

In the night his body was stolen from the palace, so that he might be buried by his followers in the rites of the eternal faith. That night Ragah heard footsteps in the street, and looking out her window saw a procession of men and women, six of whom, pallbearers, carried on their shoulders the body of a man wrapped in linen. One of the pallbearers was Nahum.

Dropping a veil over her face, Ragah left the house, and followed the procession as it moved out of the city and into Ge-Hinnom, to the rocky foothills with their olive groves. The procession halted at one of the caves in the foothills, and the pallbearers carried Simon's body inside.

From her hiding-place in an olive grove Ragah watched as the mourners wept, and collected their tears in small glass bottles, which were placed next to Simon's body. When all had paid their final respects, a huge boulder was rolled in front of the cave, blocking the entryway forever. The torches were extinguished.

Out of the darkness came the mourners' chant, the Hebrews' prayer for the dead, as old and holy as the patriarchs. The procession began to file away, Nahum one of the last to leave. She followed his departing figure with wistful eyes.

Breaking off a branch of olive leaves, Ragah went to the cave. She placed the branch in front of the boulder, and stood there quietly, wishing she could have shared in the prayers of the Hebrews.

Nahum, looking back, saw a woman standing in prayer before the boulder. Simon's widow, he thought; I will lead her back to Jerusalem. Retracing his steps, he waited respectfully for the woman to finish her prayers. Then, recognizing Ragah, he stood there as if rooted to stone.

He murmured her name. She turned in fear, but then recognized him. When he asked why she mourned for Simon, Ragah, much agitated, demanded that he let her pass. But Nahum would not, and told her he knew she was not merely an entertainer. "You have a mission," he said. "I am certain of it."

She remembered what Amyu had told her and said he must not speak to her.

"I must. Do you know I have stood in your garden, hoping you would come out so that I might talk to you?"

Ragah bent her head. "I have seen you."

Nahum asked why she had come to Ge-Hinnom.

"Because of Simon and his suffering," she answered.

"You knew him?"

"I saw him before he was killed. I heard his last scream. He was a brave man."

"May we all be as brave when our own time comes."

For the first time she looked full into Nahum's face. "May the gods spare you such a death, Nahum." Her voice was warm and filled with a womanly feeling she could no longer hide. Nahum moved forward hesitantly and held her to him for a moment.

Ragah whispered that she must go.

"Listen," said Nahum imperatively. "I must talk to you. If what I feel is true, then we are fighting for the same cause. You are more than a dancer, Ragah. I know it, I feel it!"

"I am a priestess of Aphrodite," she answered. "My goddess would not allow me to join the cause of your God."

Nahum smiled. "My God teaches that there is only one God, and He is right."

She made no reply.

Nahum began again. "I am from Jerusalem, and you from Sidon, yet there is one thing we should have in common; hatred of the Romans."

"That is true."

"Then why did you accept Pilate's golden earrings?"

"Please, Nahum," she pleaded with him, "I cannot answer your questions."

Nahum pointed to the olive grove where she had hidden. "Will you meet me here tomorrow, before the sun sets?"

Ragah did not reply. She stepped around him and hurried away, and Nahum did not follow after.

That night Nahum found no sleep. The Romans meant danger for the girl. She must and would tell him the truth. Impatiently he waited the passing of the hours.

Ragah came to the olive grove the next day, and they fell into each other's arms. They sat under an olive tree, each looked deep into the eyes of the other, and for the first time they kissed.

They met again the next afternoon, and the afternoon after that. Only one of her slave maidens knew where Ragah went during this time. Amyu did not miss her; he was busy gathering information about Pilate. The Procurator had no time for extravagant pleasures; Simon's death had spurred the rebels on and no night passed without death or arson. Pilate had other worries besides those of the underground movement. Reports came from the shores of the Sea of Galilee that another false prophet had arisen to preach against the Romans.

The lovers continued to meet, and as Ragah's love grew she could conceal her mission from him no longer.

"Pilate's golden earrings are heavy," she said, "but not so heavy that they overcome my love for you. Now how can I hate when my heart is full of love?"

"Let me take the earrings," Nahum said, "and let us leave Palestine. There are many lands Rome does not rule."

But she turned her face aside. She agreed only to allow him to be near her the night she danced for Pilate. It was Nahum's plan that night to pose as one of Pilate's musicians, and after the assassination they would escape from the palace together. Should Amyu and the Nubians offer resistance, which he doubted, Nahum's men would discourage them.

From time to time in the olive grove they had a visitor, an old shepherd named Laten, who every afternoon pastured his flock near the grove, and called them with a single note of his ram's horn. Laten was wise and knew much about the ways of God and man. He told the listening lovers of a man in Galilee who preached of love.

The words of the preacher of Galilee found an answering echo in the hearts of the young lovers. They believed in love, and as the days passed Ragah's earrings became doubly heavy as they reminded her constantly that before love lay duty.

Perhaps, she thought, the words of the preacher of Galilee are true, and we should not fight our enemy with the same weapons with which he fights us. The thought troubled her.

Amyu was growing impatient now. It was known in Jerusalem that the Procurator would soon return to Caesarea, and there was not much time remaining.

One afternoon Laten said to them, "God has changed men's hearts since I was young."

The lovers looked at him without understanding.

"Where there is love," the old shepherd said, "there should not be hate."

"In a man's heart there is room for both," said Ragah.

The shepherd smiled, and she felt uncomfortable; it was as if this old man could read her mind.

She went on: "You cannot expect us to stop hating the Romans because we love each other."

"Those who love truly cannot hate," Laten said. "The Master says this, and it is true."

"The Master," said Nahum. "Do you speak of the teacher of Galilee?"

"Yes, I speak of the man of Nazareth. He will be in Jerusalem over the Passover. Go and listen to him. You will learn how vast and deep love can grow, not only for those you love already, but for every human creature. And it is through this love that the Romans will be conquered."

Nahum shook his head bitterly. "I cannot take the Romans to my breast."

"Take them to your heart," said Laten, "and you will have conquered them. Love thy enemies, for by that love they are weakened."

Nahum laughed. "Shepherd, your thought is a beautiful one, but it has no teeth in it."

Laten only smiled gently, and after calling his flock with his ram's horn, bid them good day.

That evening Amyu was waiting for Ragah when she returned home.

The messenger from the palace had come with Pilate's summons.

The maids prepared her. Again she bathed and was massaged; perfumes, jewelry and silken clothes were laid out for her. Amyu entered as she rested, and reminded her he would await her in the garden after the deed was done.

That night the guards at the gate, recognizing the golden earrings, let her pass. In his chambers Pilate, drunk with wine and anticipation, awaited for her on his silken cushions.

He reached out to press her close to him, but she twisted away. She felt the hilt of the dagger in her belt, and it gave her courage. She said that his importunities had bruised her vanity, and asked that she be allowed to dance.

Pilate laughingly complied. As soft music drifted in from behind the curtains she began her dance, insinuatingly moving her hands over her body. Pilate groaned, his wine-heavy eyes fixed upon her, and he shouted that she dance faster for him.

Twisting to the slow rhythm of the dance, she ignored his command. Deliberately she provoked him, coming within his reach and then withdrawing quickly. Knowing that Nahum was behind the curtains among the musicians made her feel more confident. When the drums beat faster she would strike.

When the drums increased in tempo she danced near Pilate and touched the dagger at her belt, but she could not pull it forth, for it seemed as though instead of hearing the music, she heard instead the ram's horn of Laten, the shepherd, cleansing her of hatred and revenge. Then the illusion vanished, and again she danced, and once again she waited for the faster drumbeat. This time she must do what she had to do. She heard the voice of Vema, and Amyu's command, and when the drum beat faster she danced close to Pilate.

Seeing his half-closed eyes veiled with lust she gripped the dagger, but again she heard not the music but the shepherd's horn. And she hated no one, not even the Roman.

Sobbing, she dropped the dagger, and turned and ran from the room.

litter where Nahum waited, and fell into his arms. The tears were
streaming down her cheeks.
Fleeing down the corridor she heard Pilate's laughter. She ran to the
   "I could not do it," she sobbed. "Nahum, I have betrayed my people,
but at last I am free."

Nahum kissed her gently and lifted her into the litter. "Amyu will
understand," he whispered. "I will come for you before the hour."

The Nubians walked without haste to the gate, but once outside they
increased their pace through the darkened city. Pilate's guards, when the
hue and cry was raised, could find neither Ragah nor the disguised
musician in the vicinity of the palace.

Amyu was waiting for her in the garden. She brushed past him, but
he followed after and swung her around.

"What happened? Did he die?"

"No," she said. "I could not do it."

The eunuch stared at her, so angry that he could not speak. She tried
to twist away from him, but he gripped her arm and pressed her against
the garden wall.

"They were confident of you in Sidon, and so was I. Why have you
failed us? I thought the purpose of your life was to avenge your family.
I was wrong. If you failed, I should not fail to kill you. This was said
to me in Sidon. If you could not follow your orders, then I must."

Taking out a dagger from inside his tunic, Amyu plunged it into
her breast. He wept as he looked at her huddled, lifeless form.

Then he called the servants and led them from the house. They hurried through the night toward the north gate. As they passed through the
market place, Roman soldiers seized them. Amyu broke heavily away,
but one of the legionnaire's lances whistled through the air and pierced
him through the neck. He fell without a cry.

Nahum found Ragah with the dagger still in her bosom. Too stunned
to move, too crushed to weep, he sat beside her all the night, and shortly
before dawn carried her to Ge-Hinnom and into the olive grove where

they had met. When Laten the shepherd came they brought her to the foothills of the mountains, and buried her in a small cave there, after removing the dagger from her body.

Laten placed his gnarled old hand on Nahum's shoulder, and as if from a great distance Nahum heard his voice telling him that freedom had never come through violence and upheaval. Violence begot violence, the old man said, and tyranny fell of its own spiritual decay.

"You speak words," said Nahum brokenly, "words only."

"But they are truth. Ragah's mission was death. You chose death also, but then you found love together. It was love that stayed her hand."

Nahum wept upon the old man's breast.

"There is no sunlight without her," Nahum said.

Laten shook his head. "There will be the light of the sun always. Come, my young friend, I will help you close her tomb."

When this was done they spoke the prayers of death, and the shepherd said, "Here in the foothills she shall rest. Let her look to the grove where she found her happiness, and the olive trees in the sunlight will bring it back to her, even when we two are dust."

Nahum rose. "Shepherd," he said, "take me with you. Let me listen to the preacher of Nazareth."

So ends the story of Ragah, modernized and with fictional dialogue and atmosphere, but basically unchanged. As a scientist who should respect the laws of probabilities, it seems unlikely to me that the earrings found in the cave in Ge-Hinnom were those of the girl who danced for Pilate and loved a Hebrew named Nahum and died at her eunuch's hand. But Ragah's story, though probably apochryphal, and none too distinctive as a work of art, is more revealing as folklore or legend than most others I have heard or read of the time of Christ and Pilate. I thought the reader of this book, reading it in that spirit, would find the tale of interest.

» XII «

The Visitation of Enoch

I HAD not seen Munim for some years, but to me he was still my guide and mentor, the man whose influence upon me had exceeded that of any other, and I looked forward to refreshing myself at his inexhaustible fountain of spiritual riches and wisdom. I had seen and done a great deal since we last had met. No longer was I a searcher for my own life's path; I had found that path, and proved my choice a good one.

In his last letter Munim had included an enclosure that had excited my curiosity. It was a clipping from a Sudanese newspaper about an Abyssinian farmer who claimed to have seen and spoken with the Prophet Enoch. The story went on to say that eleven other Abyssinians of the same province had recently made the same claim. Munim had made no comment of his own, though I had the feeling he had sent the clipping to me for a particular reason, perhaps because our journey would be to the place where the miracle had occurred.

The story intrigued me. Enoch, son of Jared and descendant of the seven patriarchs who had followed Adam, had always been my private fascination. Among all the figures of Genesis he was one of the most remarkable. The Bible contained only scattered references to him; he had lived, so it was written, for three hundred sixty-five years, the number of days in a year. This gave to him a certain mystical significance. Genesis says of Enoch that unlike other patriarchs who "died and were not," Enoch "walked with God, and . . . God took him" (5:24).

The book of Enoch has been omitted from many modern versions of the Bible, but I had read it in its original Aramaic and Greek forms, and I was puzzled as to why, seventeen hundred years ago, officials of the Church had seen fit to remove it from general circulation. A profound scripture, it was apocalyptic in content, mystic in tone, and filled with wisdom and knowledge.

The evidence in Genesis relating to Enoch's death and immortality has given rise to much theological speculation. To many of the Christian and Jewish faith this evidence indicated that Enoch was a symbol, not a man, and had never actually lived upon the earth. The Coptic Church of Abyssinia was especially partial to this view, regarding Enoch as a supernatural messenger of God who appeared on earth shortly before the occurrence of important historical events. It was Enoch, so the Coptics believed, who had warned Noah of the coming flood, and who had proclaimed the immaculate conception of Christ to Mary. The Coptic Church held that Enoch had also appeared shortly before the fall of Jerusalem and of Rome. For these beliefs there was no practical proof, but it seemed to me that the mystery that has surrounded Enoch since the beginning of recorded history makes him one of the outstanding figures of the Genetic period before the flood.

Looking for additional information, I inquired among my friends in Jerusalem, learning that they too had heard of the miracle. Such news travels fast in the Middle East, birthplace of the three religions, where the religiously inclined are vitally interested in every kind of mystical phenomenon. The religious men, both Christian and Jew, whom I asked for an explanation were, however, reluctant to discuss the reappearance. It seemed as though I would have to wait for Munim's enlightenment.

A few days later Munim and I sat sipping coffee on the terrace of Cairo's Shepheard's Hotel. I felt he had changed greatly. Not only was he different in outward appearance, his face seamed and lined, his weight lighter; he had changed within, in the direction of quietude and withdrawal. It was not that he showed disinterest in my autobiographical details that brought him up to date, or in my questions; I had the curious impression that close as Munim had remained to the world in its practical aspects, there was a part of him that was fast retreating out of the world's reach forever.

We discussed our projected journey and Munim told me we would take the trip from Cairo to El-Shallala, from which we would go by boat up the Nile to Wadi Halfa, in the Sudan. From there the train would take us to the Sudanese twin cities of Khartoum-Omdurman, where a caravan would meet us for our journey into the Abyssinian mountains.

The river boat we boarded at El-Shallala the next day was wide and flat, driven by a revolving wheel in its stern. Munim and I were assigned to the same small cabin. There was nothing much to do, and for the first three days, as we moved slowly up the blue-gray muddy river, I watched the brilliantly colored fish as they raced the boat, the scenery of sand, palm, and rocks, the herds of crocodile bathing in the sun, the occasional Nile horses of the inhabited areas that came to drink the muddy water like huge dun cows. Monkeys, hopping through the trees, followed the boat for long distances until their shrieking parents called them home. Richly plumaged birds circled about us for hours, their fantastic colors blinding the eye. The days were hot, at least 110 degrees, but the humidity was reasonable, and it was pleasant to sit in the bow as the sun set, waiting for the night with its cooling breeze.

I saw little of Munim, who spent most of his time reading and attending to correspondence. Those few times I mentioned Enoch and the visitation to him, he quickly changed the subject. Once he said, "Patience, Paul, is a virtue in most people, but in the theologian a necessity. Exercise it, my friend, and in due time you will learn all there is to know."

The scorching sun turned our compartment on the train from Wadi Halfa to Khartoum-Omdurman into a torture chamber. Sand sifted in from the desert day and night, getting into our food, our drink, and even our conversation, until I became too miserable to observe the civilities. I sulked silently in a corner while Munim looked out upon the monotonous scene, seemingly unaffected by the heat and dirt. Visions of a cold shower haunted me; when we checked into the English Palace Hotel at Khartoum I tore off my clothes and raced into the bath.

Clean and freshly clothed, we had dinner and hired a carriage to tour the city. I was surprised to find Khartoum so modern and up to date. It seemed to me intensely British Colonial in atmosphere; more English than African. Here in the capital of the British Sudan most of the six thousand English population lived in splendid homes; and streets were wide and immaculate. Fountains, lush grass, and flowering gardens were everywhere; the African night was cool and star-bright.

The native city of Omdurman, to which we crossed next morning over the White Nile Bridge, was a considerable change. The houses on the narrow streets were made from cheap clay; the small squares were jammed with shouting Arabs. We were in the past again.

We rented three camels, boarded two, put our luggage on the other, and behind our donkey-mounted guide headed out into the desert. For twelve hours we rode without stopping while the wind blew sand into our faces. I kept my mouth and nose covered with a wool shawl Munim had given me. It was late at night when we arrived at the Abyssinian frontier station, two huts in the shade of two palm trees. Munim seemed familiar with the place; after unloading the camel we stepped into one of the huts. Too tired to eat, we prepared for bed. I fell asleep listening to the departure of the guide, with his camels, back to Omdurman.

When voices awoke me in the morning, I went outside to find Munim talking in Amharic, the native Abyssinian language, to two bearded men busily loading our luggage on donkeys.

"These are our servants, Anasius and Mulas," Munim told me. "They arrived during the night."

We breakfasted on a thick meaty soup; then we left for the second leg of our journey into the Abyssinian hills. For three days we saw nothing but sand. The constant wind, swirling it about our heads and faces, made it impossible to converse except in snatches. In any case I had the impression Munim was averse to talk. Most of the time he rode with his eyes closed, his lips moving slowly in what I deduced was a prayer. I noticed our servants were praying too. A strange and pious caravan, these four men and six donkeys trudging silently over the wasteland.

We stopped at sundown. The servants made two fires, one for Munim and myself, the other a few feet away for themselves. They cooked our meal of unhulled rice, meat, and coffee, and after the meal we sat quietly in the thick darkness of the desert night. The servants never spoke, except when Munim asked them a direct question. I was able to understand a little of what they said, since before the trip I had begun the study of Amharic.

The fourth day of our journey I noticed a sudden change in the terrain. The sand was no longer bright yellow, but brown and gray. Rocks appeared in the distance as we approached closer to the mountains. Late in the day we passed through an Abyssinian village. Half-naked children surrounded us, begging for fruit and bread. The servants gave freely to them from our provisions, bestowing with each gift a blessing.

In the mountains, scrubby trees with thick fleshy leaves were everywhere. I could see small, dilapidated farmhouses in the valleys. Cool winds chilled us by day; the nights were astonishingly cold. I had to stuff three blankets into my sleeping bag before I felt comfortable enough to fall into that relaxation that precedes sleep.

That night we stopped on a plateau, below which we could see the flickering lights of a village. The servants built a large fire, the four of us gathering around it together rather than separating into two groups as before. When Munim addressed the two servants in French they responded as perfectly as sophisticated Parisiennes. I was surprised, but reluctant to ask questions. After the evening meal I gingerly reopened the matter of Enoch.

Munim smiled. "I know little more than you, my friend. I have come here to find out more."

"How are you going to go about it?"

"We will go to the village of this man who claims to have seen and spoken with Enoch; it is the site of one of our important monasteries. The Church Synod in Addis Ababa has asked me to interrogate him there. Trials of the other eleven claiming to have seen Enoch have been completed; I have documented the evidence. I am to hold the final ecclesiastic trial and interrogation, and from the evidence am to determine whether this last man is telling the truth. I am also to write a summation on the entire matter."

I lit a cigarette impatiently. "How can what this man says be the truth?"

"It has happened before," said Anasius, the servant, quietly.

"To a simple farmer?" I scoffed.

"Most of the apostles were but simple fishermen," Anasius replied.

"Now that the twelve apostles have been mentioned," said Munim, "let me remind you of the twelve different reports of Enoch's reappearance."

"In twelve different towns and villages," added Anasius.

Mulas said: "And always at the twelfth hour."

It was all too incredible for me. "I cannot," I said, "bring myself to believe it."

"No one is asking you to," said Munim. "None of us should reach a conclusion until after the trial." He rose from the ground. "Tomorrow will be a busy day. We must get some sleep. Goodnight, my brothers," he said to the servants.

"May God be with you, Ras Munim," they replied.

When we were settled in our sleeping bags I asked Munim, "Tell me, why did you invite me to go along on this trip? I've been curious."

"Because, Paul, I felt that more than any of my friends you could profit most from it. I know you are a scientist, and the scientist of course is the man of reason. But you are that strange amalgam: the scientist who has been touched by the hand of fate and made intuitive and aware beyond the lot of other men. I recognized this the moment we met, and over the years I have hoped that this intuitive quality that so distinguishes you would, perhaps, develop in the direction of religion. I am putting it badly, Paul; I mean both more and less than what I say. But I felt that we are concerned in this trial with the most important and revealing spiritual event ever to be witnessed by a man in the twentieth century, and it was you I wanted to share it with me."

I felt humble before this spiritual man who had found in me some infinitesimal trace of that divine fire and grace that animated his every word and act and gesture. After a moment I asked about Anasius and Mulas; why tonight they had eaten with us for the first time, and why he had called them his brothers.

"They are Coptic priests," he said, "extremely intelligent men schooled in Cairo and France and deeply versed in theology and religion. Anasius has written a book that will live long after we are dead; one of the classics in its field. Mulas is a man much beloved by all who know him. But when both men were ordained they considered themselves unworthy to serve God, and so they are learning humility by first learning to serve men. In their role of servants they must obey; but as priests and men they are my brethren. They are going home to their monastery, which we will reach tomorrow."

"I noticed they called you not 'Brother' but 'Ras.' Isn't 'Ras' an Abyssinian title of honor?"

"They called me 'Ras,' Paul, because I am a Bishop. I neglected to tell you that before," and so saying, Munim rolled over and went to sleep.

For a long time I lay awake watching this man who had never ceased to amaze me. I had laughed and joked with him, bothered him with my petty worries and concerns. And now I found him to be a prince of his church. I wondered if I could ever relax with him again, this Bishop in a sleeping bag.

I opened my eyes the next morning to see Munim standing at the fire, watching our two priest-servants brewing coffee. Before I could roll up my sleeping bag, Anasius was at my side, busy at the task. We finished breakfast, mounted the donkeys, and continued our journey through the mountains.

Toward sundown we arrived at the small monastery which Munim that afternoon had announced was our first destination. An ancient monk greeted us at the door. We were taken directly to a washing room, where buckets of cold water were set out for us. Following Munim's example, I washed my hands, face, and feet. Waiting for us in the refectory were fourteen monks of the monastery, including Anasius and Mulas, now dressed in the black sackcloth garments of the Coptic priesthood. Prayers were said, and we sat down to a meal of bread, goat cheese, and water.

The meal was eaten in silence; prayers were said again, and Munim and I went outside into the garden.

"Is this where the interrogation will be held?" I asked him.

"No. We have stopped here tonight because a new prior of the monastery will be chosen, and I have been asked to witness the ceremony."

Munim showed me around the grounds. The monastery had been built directly into the mountainside; space was at a premium and everything — rooms, corridors, furnishings — were on a surprisingly small scale. The monks' beds looked to me like coffins. I remarked upon it.

"They are," Munim said, and explained to me that the Coptic monk, who is always prepared for death, looks upon the coffin as his eternal resting place.

The walls of the tiny chapel were of rough stone; its floor stamped yellow earth. On the altar were an embroidered cloth of red and gold, the Coptic cross, and two small glass bowls. Behind the altar hung two paintings, one of the lion of David, the other of the Virgin with Child. They were primitively executed, but impressive in their strength and boldness. High up on one of the walls was a long, narrow window of inexpensive glass, with a bench directly beneath it. Otherwise the chapel was bare.

The tour completed, Munim led me to a dormitory room with a single cot, washstand, and ewer of water. The ceremony would begin before dawn, he explained, and I should try to get some sleep. The day had been a long one; I found no difficulty in dozing off, and awoke to Munim's hand shaking my shoulder gently. "We are ready," he said.

In the chapel a length of dark material had been hung over the window, shutting out the moonlight, and the room was totally dark except for the amber lights glowing weakly in the altar bowls. We sat down on the bench. From the corridor I could hear the shuffling of feet, and then the monks slowly entered, the aged prior leading the procession. The monks' hoods hid their faces completely; only the prior's face was uncovered.

Seven times the prior led the monks around the chapel; when the procession halted each monk turned around seven times in his place. Then each monk knelt where he stood, some near the bench, some near the altar, some isolated in the corners.

In an eerie silence the prior came to stand before the bench where Munim and I were sitting. He began to pray loudly in Amharic, and the monks joined him. The chapel reverberated with the sound, and I felt restless and uncomfortable. This continued for almost an hour, when the prayers suddenly stopped. From somewhere outside I heard the silvery echo of the chapel bells.

The silence and strain were unbearable. I found it difficult to breathe or swallow. Across the chapel the two dim altar lamps spluttered with a crackling that sounded loud as rifle fire. I imagined I heard other strange noises, but nothing in the shadows moved.

Munim, whose head was bowed, seemed far away from me, and I tried desperately to occupy my mind. I ran through the street names of Jerusalem; tried to recall the title of every book I had read; but they were a jumble in my mind. When I felt I could stand the silence no longer, the prior resumed his prayers.

Again the monks responded, but this time in a cadenced chanting of Amharic and Greek. Its effect was lulling and soporific, and gradually my strain and tension vanished. The chanting ceased, and in the renewed silence I felt a quietness, brooding and vast. I thought how strange it was that I should be here, in the strange loneliness of the Abyssinian mountains, and tried to visualize what would have been the reaction of people in Paris, London, New York, or Delhi to the remarkable fact that, thousands of miles away from each of these cities, fourteen monks knelt in darkness atop an Ethiopian mountain waiting for God to choose one of their number.

I was deeply impressed by the unshakable faith of these men who believed this night that the Creator watched them, heard their prayers, and would select from among them their new leader. There came to me now a perception of that great and majestic aspect of Christianity in which there was oneness with the Almighty of the most lowly, and in this moment I found myself in full accord with these simple men. I was certain God would give them a sign. I thought of how my own life and career had been shaped by the inspiration and example of religious men — Munim, Flinders Petrie, the old sheik in El-Shallala. All three were men who prayed; I felt I wanted to pray for them, to appeal to Heaven that these men be blessed.

The prior's voice broke suddenly into my thoughts; he and the monks were praying once again. The litany was brief and I was surprised it ended so quickly. The silence that followed was subtly different; I sensed in it an expectation, an assurance of something about to occur.

It was then it happened. A ray from the rising sun pierced the dark chapel. The cloth covering the window had a small hole in its center, and as I watched the beam grew stronger, traveling like a finger of heaven across the chapel floor. It went directly to the breast of one of the kneeling monks near the altar, suffusing him in what seemed a bright and holy glow.

The prior said, "Praise the Lord."

"Amen," the monks responded.

Hurrying to the chosen monk, the prior bid him rise, and lifting his hood, kissed his cheek. Not until the prior stepped aside did I see that the new prior was our humble servant Anasius.

I waited till Munim and the other monks had given Anasius their fraternal blessing, and went to him. On his face there was a look not of pride or satisfaction, but of devout and humble acceptance of the new responsibilities vouchsafed to him by God Himself.

Munim was at my side. "We will breakfast now, if you are ready, and be on our way."

It was only a half day's trip to our final destination, a village, Munim assured me, as old as the world itself. This was easy to believe; in the fields I saw farmers working plows so ancient that in any museum they would have been archaeological treasures. The village itself was large, with around two thousand population. None of its inhabitants, Munim told me, had ever had any contact with the outside world. Only the monks of the monastery had traveled.

The monastery was the headquarters of this unique, self-supporting community. A great stone building with several wings, it was the village's town hall, school, and administrative center; outside I saw villagers waiting for an audience with the prior and his officials. Munim introduced me to the kindly prior and I was shown to a well-furnished room with bath and shower. Delighted, I soaked for an hour and shaved for the first time in eight days.

When Munim knocked on my door I scarcely recognized him. He was mitred and in his Bishop's robes, with lace at his wrists and around his shoulders. A band of ermine fringed his cape, the lapels of which sparkled with precious stones. On the index finger of his right hand was a heavy gold ring.

He smiled at my amazement, and put his arm around my shoulder as if to reassure me that despite all this ecclesiastical finery he was still the same old Munim, and my friend.

"The interrogation is about to begin," he told me. "There is a seat for you at the dais. The man I will question, Rada Salas, is fifty years old and has lived here all his life. He has one wife and three children. He owns a small farm where he raises just enough to provide for his family, and his wife weaves cloth that is sold in the village market place. Salas' education is limited — he has had only a few years of schooling here at the monastery — but he can read and write. He is respected by the monks and villagers and has lived a very uneventful life. Another point: he knows nothing of the eleven other appearances of Enoch. Our monks had strict orders not to speak of them to him or to any of the villagers."

The interrogation hall was crowded with fifty or sixty people of the town. Though it was still daylight, gasoline lamps burned in brackets on the wall. At a long table in front of the room sat six men, four monks and two elders from the village. As we entered, the entire room rose in respect to Munim, who went directly to the center chair at the table. I took a chair at the end.

When Rada Salas was brought in I saw he was in every respect as Munim had described him — a simple and humble farmer. His dark eyes held a determined gleam, as though he knew there were skeptics at this, his great trial, and he meant to be believed. Munim extended his hand for Salas to kiss his ring as an oath of honesty, and Salas took his seat before the dais.

Munim was aloof and distant. "Salas," he began, "tell me freely what happened that has brought you before this court."

"It happened shortly before the third hour some three weeks ago," said Salas. "The day was hot and I left my fields early for the noon meal. After eating I went to my room to pray, but this day I was tired and did not feel like praying. I could not concentrate on the words.

"But for a long time I knelt there, and suddenly I had the feeling I was not alone. Thinking it was one of the children, I turned, ready to scold for being interrupted. But there was no one there. I returned to my prayers, but the feeling that I was not alone returned to me. And then I felt a hand on my shoulder. I looked up, and that was when I saw him."

"How did he look?" asked Munim.

"He was old," said Salas. "He had white hair and a white beard. He wore a white garment without sandals. His skin was smooth and his eyes were dark and clear."

"And then?"

"I stood up," answered Salas. "I asked 'Who are you?' and he replied, 'You know who I am. I am always in your heart and often on your lips.' Then I knew it was Enoch. I began to kneel, but he took me by the shoulders and would not let me. He said to me: 'I have come to ask you, Rada Salas, if in your heart you believe the world is ready for the fulfillment of the peace.'

"I did not know what to answer, and I asked, 'Why do you put this question to me? I am a simple farmer and an ignorant man. Go to the monastery, where the wise men are.'"

The villagers leaned forward intently, and the men at the dais were observing Salas with narrowed eyes. Only Munim seemed completely composed, unaffected either by credulity or skepticism.

"Then," continued Salas, "the man I believed to be Enoch said to me, 'I have asked you, Rada Salas. You can answer. Think upon it, and I will return.' And then he vanished."

"What did you do then?" asked Munim.

"I was afraid. I thought I had been dreaming but knew this was not so. I asked my wife if she had seen anyone enter the house and she shook her head. I stepped outside, but saw no one. I took a drink of water to clear my head, but the man would not leave my mind. In the fields I tried to work, but it was useless. Before the sun set that day I came here to the monastery and told the prior everything."

The elderly prior rose from his chair. "What Salas has told you is the same in every respect as what he told me that evening." He addressed himself to Munim: "The same morning I received from Addis Ababa, from the Mother Church, the secret report of the eleven other appearances. So I questioned Salas thoroughly. I thought it best for him to spend the night at the monastery. I instructed several monks to spend the night with me in the presence of Salas. In my room we began our prayers and continued for several hours."

"Did you sleep?" inquired Munim.

The prior shook his head. "Only Salas slept from time to time. It was four in the morning when he roused and sat up."

The prior gestured to Salas, who said, "I felt again the presence of the stranger, but was unable to rise. I felt a breath on the back of my neck, and knew Enoch had returned.

· 239 ·

"Did you see anyone?" Munim asked the prior.

"No one."

"Nor did I see anyone," Salas continued, "though I heard Enoch's voice. He asked me again if I thought the world was ready for the fulfillment of the peace. I could not answer him, yet I knew I must, and the words when they came seemed to arise from somewhere deep inside me. I said, 'I cannot explain why, Enoch, yet I feel the world is ripe for the fulfillment, though millions of hearts must be broken for it.' "

The prior said, "Those are the words we heard Salas say."

"I heard Enoch say to me," continued Salas, " 'It is as John wrote. As the world was destroyed by water, so it must be destroyed by fire before Jehovah will grant peace.' "

"None of us heard the reply of the man said to be Enoch," the prior said.

Leaning forward, Munim questioned the farmer in such detail that I thought surely the man would become confused. For over an hour Munim continued, but Salas answered exactly as before. At last Munim stood and told Salas he was free to go. I waited until my friend left the hall, and then rose from the table with the others. The trial had deeply impressed me and I wanted to be alone to think it over. As I passed down the corridor, Munim called to me through his open door.

Still dressed in his magnificent robes, he stood at the window overlooking the village. He turned to me, and in his eyes was a question.

"I still can't believe Salas saw or heard Enoch," I said, "but yet Salas is no liar."

There was no reply from Munim.

"What did Salas mean by the fulfillment of the peace?" I asked.

"The millenium mentioned in Revelation — the thousand years of peace before the end of the world."

"Salas also mentioned destruction by fire."

"That is in the Apocalypse of John the Evangelist."

"Couldn't Salas have read Revelation in the New Testament?"

"Possibly," said Munim, "though he knows only the rudiments of

reading. And possibly he could have heard of both from the monks."
He sighed. "But the incredible fact is that Salas' testimony is precisely
the same as that given by the eleven other men who claim to have seen
Enoch."

"Could Salas have talked with these men?"

"Impossible. It is true that the Sudanese newspaper clipping I sent
to you mentioned the other appearances that took place elsewhere in
the province, but there is no possibility that this news could have traveled here by word of mouth."

I shrugged helplessly.

Talking aloud to himself Munim said, "If Enoch did appear to Salas
in the monastery, why was he not heard also by the prior and the monks?
Why has he been seen only by the twelve men?"

In Munim's face skepticism still warred with a desire to believe, yet
there was a new emotion there: anguish. I said, "Perhaps there was no
actual appearance, and the explanation lies in the realm of hallucina-
tion. The twelve may have had such strong and overwhelming thoughts
of Enoch that in some mystical manner they projected through their
vision to God Himself."

"I wish that were the solution, but it is not. The witnessing of Enoch
by twelve different men is no coincidence; but it is also no miracle. Let
me pray, Paul; perhaps enlightenment will come."

The next morning when I asked for Munim I was told that the Bishop
was still in seclusion and could not be disturbed. It was noon when I
saw him again. The anguish I had noticed yesterday had sunk his eyes
deep into their sockets, and his face seemed noticeably more lined. His
whole aspect expressed hopelessness and resignation. He spoke to me
lucidly enough, but I felt his thoughts were far away.

I asked him about his report and he had finally come to a conclusion.
I knew that like myself he could not accept Salas' story. The answer, I
thought, lay probably within the vivid imagination of Salas, who had all
his life been trained to think and feel within the framework of his
mystical religious belief. The fact that eleven other men had had the

same vision could, and must, be explained by the laws of probability.

"I have come to no conclusion," Munim said. "And yet I ask myself, if this was only a vision, are not visions the inspirational events of the history of mankind? Is not religion based upon visual phenomena? Abraham had a vision of his God; Moses heard his Lord's voice when the bush burned and was not consumed; Jesus heard the voice of Satan on the Mount of Temptation.

"Unlike your science of archaeology, which is able to prove the material facts of religion, religion as belief is but a vision, and as such the greatest gift human beings have received. I believe the appearance of Enoch was an expression of God. It has both reason and purpose, though I cannot as yet understand that reason and purpose, and do not pretend to.

"Those who took unto them the words of Jesus were the simple ones. 'Suffer the little children to come unto me, and forbid them not; for of such is the kingdom of heaven.' 'Such is the kingdom of heaven,'" he repeated. "Jesus' words are understandable only in the light of his symbols. The souls of children are not warped and twisted by the passions of men or their ordeals or their struggles. These twelve peasants have the souls of children, and such are the souls that receive divine knowledge.

"I know one thing, Paul. Salas' trial has taught me my greatest lesson. I have dedicated my entire life to God, yet now I have learned I am not worthy to serve him. It was not I who received Enoch's message, for I was unready for it. Sitting there, dressed in my pompous vestments, I felt as a Bishop of my Church, not as the humble servitor. I have been ordained by men and not by God.

"Paul, I shall not return with you to Cairo. I have decided to live as a mendicant monk in the mountains of my native land. It is there I will search for God. Perhaps, when I have learned humility, He will come to me."

He made a gesture with his hand, and I understood he wished me to leave him.

Munim did not appear for the evening meal in the dining hall, and I did not see him again till sundown, when the air was cool enough to begin my journey home. Two servants were to accompany me to the Sudanese border, where a guide with camels would meet and escort me back to Omdurman.

Munim came up to me wearing his ordinary black robe. He took my hand. "Goodbye, Paul, and God bless you. Don't worry about me. One day I may return to the world, though that day may never come. I leave it to God."

He signaled the servants and the donkey caravan started down the hill. I looked back to see Munim still standing at the monastery door.

And so he departed from my life. I never saw or heard from him again. He was lost to me and to all those of the outside world who loved and revered him. Perhaps Munim was a casualty of Mussolini's rape of Abyssinia or of the world war that followed, prophesied by Enoch to a simple farmer that strange day so many years ago. I do not know and will never know. But he is always with me in my prayers, when I ask God to grant to Munim his special grace.

Facts About
the Ilton "Salome"

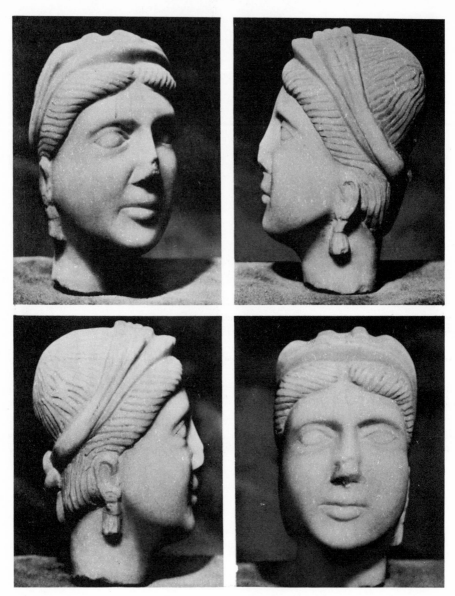

Four views of "Salome."

The Ilton "Salome"

Height: 4 1/10 inches
Material: White marble
Patina: Ivory-like
Condition: Excellent except for mutilated nose
Workmanship: Syrian or Palestinian, with strong Hellenistic influences
Sculptor: Unknown
Age: From period between 4 and 39 A.D., approximately
Subject: A young woman of royal rank
Found: In a Roman pottery wine jar, near Tiberias on the Sea of Galilee,
      Palestine. The jar is now in Rockefeller Museum, Jerusalem
Identification clues:
1. It is a portrait of a definite person, not an idol or statue of an idealized goddess.
2. A portrait of a young woman of royal rank, therefore a princess or queen.
3. Found near ruins of palace of Herod Antipas, who beheaded John the Baptist in 32 A.D., and where Salome lived.
4. Strongly sensuous personality of the subject fits known character of Salome.
5. No other princess of the time or sufficient importance to merit a portrait in a region where such portraits were rarely made is known to us by name or history.

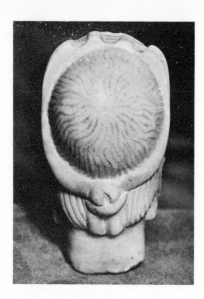

Back view of "Salome."

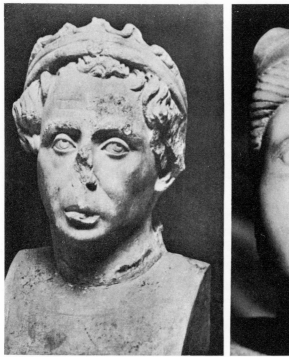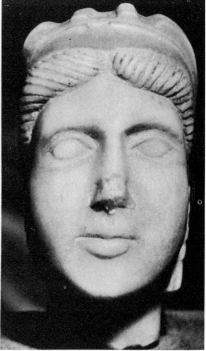

Comparison of indented diadems signifying royal or imperial rank of wearers. Subject on left in Alexandria Museum, identified as a priest of the imperial cult (proof is indented shape of diadem). Note similar indentations on upper part of "Salome" diadem.

Highlights from

the Fabulous Ilton Collection

While it would be impossible to include a photograph of every object in Paul Ilton's extensive collection, the publishers have included here several illustrations which may interest the reader.

Life size wood mask from mummy case of Queen Hatchepsut with original traces of color; holes indicate presence of copper nails with which mask was fastened to outer case; 1200 B.C.

Black granite incense holder; Assyrian; in phallic shape; 9″ high; from Aleppo, Syria, near ruins of Assyrian Temple; bears some strange cuneiform letters on base; finely carved bearded heads of priests on sides; 1000 B.C.

Black soft stone amulet with early Semitic writing; actual size; found near Hebron; from time of Moses, about 1200 B.C.

Bronze Sistrum; Egyptian; 4¼" high, 2⅛" wide; Isis head on front and back flanked by Uraeus snakes; handle and upper section lacking; from Megiddo, Palestine; 1300 B.C.

· 251 ·

Rare group of six gold pieces, actual size; Babylonian priest's breast decoration, composed of two square-shaped gold leaves engraved with two bearded heads, pomegranate tree and bird; two gold pins in form of lotus flowers; gold plate with geometric designs, and gold crescent moon ornament with two original garnets at each tip and square-cut emerald in center; all from Babylonian Period.

Group of gold jewelry, dating between 200 B.C. and 400 A.D.; actual size.

· 253 ·

*Rakka handled bowl; 6" diameter, 4½"
deep; blue with silver iridescence; from
Kufr el-Cana, Palestine; 1000 A.D.*

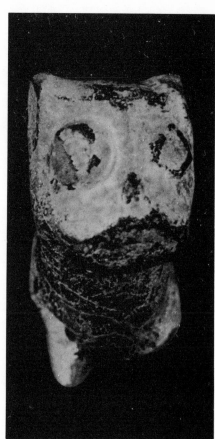

*Rakka cat head; actual size; fine sil-
ver and gold iridescence; one of rar-
est and most unusual Rakka pieces
ever discovered; probably only existing Rakka animal figure; from Kufr
el-Cana, Palestine; 1000 A.D.*

Limestone tomb plate from tomb near Gaza, Palestine, showing traces of original red coloring; represents two praying men with raised hands; hieroglyphic inscription imploring assistance of gods for deceased; found in one of rare Egyptian tombs in Palestine; 700–500 B.C.